PRAISE FOR *OUTSOURCE SMART*

"*Outsource Smart* is a solid account of what it takes to build a thriving business using virtual resources."

—Paul Lemberg, business strategist

"In a modern world of 'Fake Work' being performed by a disengaged workforce, outsourcing done 'right' is just a smart and effective way to get things done. Daven Michaels has mastered this skill and can guide you to do the same!"

—Joe Polish, president, Piranha Marketing

"Every entrepreneur struggling with overwhelm needs to read *Outsource Smart*. This is the first practical, behind-the-scenes look at the outsourcing industry from the entrepreneur's perspective."

—Marshall Sylver, educator, entertainer, and author

"Hope is not a good business strategy! The point is, if you want business or life success, it's time to stop wishing for success and start working for success. It's the only way to get the comfort and security you deserve. Put Daven Michaels on your team; you'll be glad you did."

—Ted Thomas, America's Tax Lien Certificate and Tax Deed Authority

"*Outsource Smart* is a must read for someone wanting to live the laptop lifestyle."

—Mike Filsaime, Internet marketing expert

D1495241

"This book gives you great ideas and strategies to save time and money, and serve your customers better than you could trying to do it all by yourself."
        —Brian Tracy, author of *Now, Build a Great Business*

"This book is fantastic. It is a must read for anyone who wants to conquer the world of business today. The lesson here is that you cannot do it on your own. Daven shows the small business person how to compete with the big boys and win. He's my brother from another mother, a dear friend and colleague."
        —Les Brown, motivational speaker

"If you are interested in working smart, achieving more, and joining the growing ranks of successful 'Laptop Entrepreneurs,' make sure you read Daven Michaels' outstanding book, *Outsource Smart*."
        —Mark Anastasi, author of the *New York Times* best seller *The Laptop Millionaire*

"Daven is one of the sharpest guys I know in the outsourcing industry! *Outsource Smart* is a must read if you are serious about lowering costs, increasing productivity and raising profits!"
        —Bill Walsh, America's business expert CEO/Founder, Powerteam International

Outsource Smart

**Be Your Own Boss ...
Without Letting Your Business
Be the Boss of You**

Daven Michaels

MAR 19 2013

PROPERTY OF
SENECA COLLEGE
LIBRARIES
NEWNHAM CAMPUS

WITHDRAWN

NEW YORK   CHICAGO   SAN FRANCISCO
LISBON   LONDON   MADRID   MEXICO CITY   MILAN
NEW DELHI   SAN JUAN   SEOUL   SINGAPORE
SYDNEY   TORONTO

The **McGraw·Hill** Companies

Copyright © 2013 by Daven Michaels. All rights reserved. Printed in the United States of America. Except as permitted under the United States Copyright Act of 1976, no part of this publication may be reproduced or distributed in any form or by any means, or stored in a database or retrieval system, without the prior written permission of the publisher.

1 2 3 4 5 6 7 8 9 10   DOC/DOC 1 8 7 6 5 4 3 2

ISBN   978-0-07-179979-9
MHID   0-07-179979-6

e-ISBN   0-07-179980-5
e-MHID 0-07-179980-X

Library of Congress Cataloging-in-Publication Data

Michaels, Daven
   Outsource smart : be your own boss—without letting your business become the boss of you / by Daven Michaels.
      p. cm.
   ISBN 978-0-07-179979-9 (alk. paper)—ISBN 0-07-179979-6 (alk. paper)
1. Contracting out. I. Title.
   HD2365.M53 2013
   658.4'058—dc23   2012034097

McGraw-Hill books are available at special quantity discounts to use as premiums and sales promotions or for use in corporate training programs. To contact a representative, please e-mail us at bulksales@mcgraw-hill.com.

This book is printed on acid-free paper.

Outsource Smart, although written as a roadmap for you, the business person, was also a labor of love. I was inspired by the desire to unshackle and inspire those who continue to struggle; working long hours for less than they deserve. There is a way out. I've found it and I want to share what I've learned with you, just as mentors and friends have contributed to my growth and supported me over the years.

I Dedicate This Book to . . .
Ian Rich, for giving me the keys to the kingdom.
Chris Johns, for unlocking the door to the kingdom.
Beejal Parmar, for helping me rule the kingdom.
Liz, for teaching me the ways of love.
Marilyn, Damian, Chase, Chantal & Jocelyn, for their inspiration.
My mom, for her discipline, dedication & love.
Dave, for giving me my voice.
Dad, for making me the man I am today.
And to you, the reader, for allowing me to contribute.

Your Devoted Fan,
Daven Michaels

CONTENTS

FOREWORD

JAY CONRAD LEVINSON,
AUTHOR OF *GUERRILLA MARKETING*

Over the last 40 years, I've authored or coauthored 58 books published in 62 languages and sold 21 million copies. One of my most well-known books, *Guerrilla Marketing*, introduces a body of unconventional ways of pursuing conventional goals. It's a proven method of achieving profits with minimum money.

Outsource Smart by Daven Michaels accomplishes the same thing in a way that's revolutionizing the way people do business. Don't read this book; *devour* it. Outsourcing your tasks and running your business by accessing the support of VAs (virtual assistants) will not only free you to use your time doing things you'd rather be doing, but it will also propel you to pursue your dreams.

Daven doesn't just tell you how to outsource. His candor and straightforward approach offers a blueprint for simplifying your life and streamlining your business by delegating specific tasks to qualified service providers.

As Daven points out throughout his book, there has never been a better time to start your own business. If you're already self-employed, there's never been a better time to rise to the next level. Outsourcing will support you either way. These fruitful times are breeding thousands of service providers and VAs all over the planet—each with a variety of skills and talents. *Outsource Smart* shows you how to avail yourself of their services and once you do, how to create the infrastructure that will support your business.

The twenty-first-century entrepreneurial paradigm is in many ways the same as it's always been: recognizing opportunities and understanding how and when to capitalize on them. The difference is that today we act more quickly, make faster decisions and risk more easily than others who would rather cling to the pseudo-safety of a nine-to-five job, with or without a 401K.

About a decade ago, only a very few could have imagined the impact made by the Internet on the global economy in today's marketplace. Opportunities have expanded and new industries have come to life—industries that didn't exist until the new world grew around them. Again, similar possibilities are being created by the outsourcing industry. Boundless success and wealth await entrepreneurs with the foresight to capitalize on these opportunities.

Today's economy is ripe for the development of new business. Contemporary entrepreneurs see the light at the end of the tunnel and a VA is likely holding that light.

Because of big business downsizing, decentralization, relaxation of government regulations, affordable technology, and a revolution in consciousness, people around the world are gravitating to small business in record numbers. *Outsource Smart* will help guide your business into the new economy. The insights and resources Daven Michaels shares are invaluable, whether you're just starting out or you've been around awhile and you're ready to do things differently.

Just as *Guerrilla Marketing* has been proven in action to work for small businesses around the world because it's simple to understand, easy to implement, and outrageously inexpensive, *Outsource Smart* teaches methods of making more money in less time through the art of delegation. The investment is small, but it pays big dividends in the long run.

ACKNOWLEDGMENTS

I'd like to give special thanks to the following people for their friendship, love, and support . . .

my agent, Wendy Keller,

my editor, Donya Dickerson,

my maker, . . . and my dearest friends and colleagues without whom, I would be nothing: Chris Crandall, LJ Gacho, William Spies, Mary Glorfield, Richard and Veronica Tan, Ken McArthur, Tony Alusi, Bryan Johns, Alec Call, Hal Linden, Pina De Rosa, Stephanie Graziano, Edward Niu, Paul Fishkind, Bill McIntosh Moe, June, Liz, Dani and Brook Claman, Holly and Jim Freeman, Jim Cole, Beatrice Morris, Bill and Shoshana Sheinberg, Stephen Gelber, Jeff Kepnes, Brad Fallon, Blake Goodwin, Larry Loik, Larry Benet, Canyon Schaub, Marco and Fe Cervoni, Fe and Joey Wachs, JP and Robin Cervoni, Steve and Robyn Love, Wayne Deehring, Tim McCoy, Kristin McCoy, Dave Arsanow, Dr. Emma Jean Thompson, Rebecca Keller, Rob Dorival, James and Shilo Downey, Carole Hodges, Angie Granger, Rene Kamstra, Jerome Vaultier, Sandy Sandler, Alka Dalal, Christine Lee, Maria Turnbloom, Sloan and Stephanie Hales, Kristi Reyes, Susy Lau, Jennifer Noguera, Gina Dayao, Jim Argue, Melissa Kaplan, Ellen Salashette, Todd Brown, Jennifer Kaplan, Yogi, Shivani and Kushi Parmar, Lili and Howard Landman, Jim Mihaley, Josh Spoon, Gail Kingsbury, Les Brown, Mark Victor Hansen, Jack Canfield, Tony Robbins, Marshall and Erica Sylver, Jon Talarico,

Robert Finkelstein, Michael Stein, Canyon Schaub, Larry Goins, Ed Diamond, Joey Montez, Stefanie and Tania Hartman, Martin Howey, Chris Wise, Emunah Malinovitz, Chris and Nicola Lee, Dave Glickman, Mirah Macaorao, Aubrey Diaz, Dustin Mathews, AJ Puedan, Greg Writer, Jeff Mills, Damien Zamora, Frank Sousa, Lee Arnold, Moody Igram, Giles Steinberg, Tom Beal, Mike Evans, Mike Filsaime, Cleo Babilonia, Christian Banister, Meredith Childers, Marco and Denise Bello, Alissa Beale, Mark Barakat, Beej Von Ryan, Steve and Josh Belasco, Doug Bench, Ori Bengal, George Benitez, Aaron Tardos, Gary and Shirley Benton, Ted and Honey Cohen, Michael Binikos, Desiree Robbins, Chris Howard, Dan Birnbaum, Raven Blair, Mike Blaha, Gary Blitz, Phoren A. Fare, Michelle Blake, Jerry Andrews, Dimitri Craven, Brendon Burchard, Andy Boettner, Marilyn Kronmal, Kim Mendoza, Lucie Knight, Marc Kossmann, Charlie Seymour Jr., Ted Thomas, Les Brown, John Leslie Brown, Michelle Hayes, Darrin Mish, Leila Steinberg, Mike Lathigee, James Malinchak, Colin Daymude, Solomon Mansoor, "Coach" Pat Martin, Clate Mask, Lisa McCarthy, Dan McCormick, Cel Mercado, Rat Metz, Mark Barakat, Debbie Montis, Matt Morris, Dorit Genazzani, Miki Nitzani, Maret, Kris and Micah Orlis, Orestes Matacena, Orna Rachovitsky, Casey Eberhart, David Bouford, Rick Dearr, Pasquale Rotella, Reza Gerami, Robert Polinkas, Joe Polish, Larry Pollack, Rick Powell, Rochelle O'Donnel, The Keymer Twins, Melody and Marilyn, Ted Harper, Adam Salis, Sarah and David Scher, Sam Bell, Tyrone Shum, Harold Smith, Steve Stern, Emerald Tapley, Ruben Rivera, Jerry Andrews, Kele Ward, Ira Unterman, Chris Wayne, Wade Randolph Hampton, Bill Walsh, Greg Wasik, Neil Ward, Greig Wells, Peter Wolfing, Mike Wooming, Brad Baker, Bobby Zeitler, Adam Horwitz, Berny Dohrman, Lisa Nochols, Alex Carroll, Alicia and Larett Lyttle, Mike Koenig, Chris Curtin, Jack Bosch, Russell Brunson, Christine Comaford, Raymond Aaron, Travis Campbell, Ross Hamilton, Ross Hamilton, Mike Warren, Armand Morin, Mark Anastasi, Paul Lemberg, Sam Khorramian, David Cavanagh, Joel Therien, Mark Call, and Christina Littrell Williams.

INTRODUCTION

CHANGING TIMES

IS THIS THE AMERICAN DREAM?

The American dream has become a nightmare. I don't know about you, but sometimes it makes me scream. Technological advances over the last 40 years have put opportunities once reserved for large corporations and the rich into the hands of ordinary citizens. Small businesses and sole proprietorships have grown in direct proportion to these advances. The caveat: these same technological advances meant to liberate us have buried most of us.

Remember when we thought technology would do some of our work for us, allowing us more free time to live the "good life"? Consider recent technologies intended to speed up productivity and streamline business, such as e-mail, texting, Skype, and social media. Have these platforms truly given us more time away from menial tasks, or have they added to our workload?

Technology as Tyrant

After starting a business in search of autonomy, many disillusioned small business owners end up being chained to their businesses, working for what averages out to $6 per hour. People who wanted to be their own bosses have found they now have a tyrant for a boss: the technology they'd thought would free them.

Remember when the fax machine came onto the scene? It was a tool meant to speed up the delivery of information. On one hand, fax machines allowed for greater efficiency. We were able to send proposals to prospective clients and respond rapidly to requests for information.

On the other hand, the new technology became a monster, feeding into society's insatiable appetite for immediate gratification by training customers and clients to *expect* faster turnaround time, and by placing more pressure on the person required to deliver the information.

The face of communication continued to evolve as we progressed from land lines to pagers to cell phones and, now, to smart phones. With technology exploding at its present rate, it's practically impossible to hide. We're continuously held to higher expectations, aware that if we don't toe the line, our clients will move on. In many cases, the confidence and self-assurance once the hallmark of the modern businessperson have been reduced to a fear-based mentality governed by the stress of doing business under these conditions.

What's happening is this: workloads that were supposed to decrease as technological advancements increased find us overworked, overwhelmed, and overcome by stress. That good old-fashioned work ethic ingrained in us by past generations has many people by the neck, eyes bulging, unsure how to break loose and stop the insanity.

As a businessman who took himself from zero to hero in eight years, I learned fast that the key to successful entrepreneurship is working *smarter* instead of harder.

This is a great concept for those who have the budget to hire a support staff. But given America's current small-business-resistant economic climate, where liabilities, taxes, holiday pay, vacation pay, sick pay, health insurance, 401Ks, and other expenses make it extremely difficult to hire, most small businesses are severely understaffed. And the exhausted entrepreneur cannot imagine taking time to interview, hire, process the paperwork for, and then train a new employee—better to work harder, not smarter, and just get by until "things get better." Chances are this shortsighted approach means things will *never* get better.

MAKING THINGS BETTER: MY STORY

Before I start telling you how to improve your life, I should probably tell you how I improved mine. I learned to work smarter, not harder, well, the hard way.

You hear a lot of entrepreneurs talk about the *school of hard knocks*. It was my alma mater, too. But the knocks aren't quite as hard when you allow yourself to do something (1) you have a natural affinity for, and (2) you enjoy. I was lucky in that I had parents who believed in the "do what you love and the money will follow" mantra and taught it to me.

I began working at 13, started a business at 17, and by the time I was in my mid-twenties, I had made my first million. Almost 30 years ago, I stood alone behind the cash register of my first business: a retail clothing store in Hollywood, California. After five days without a single sale, visions of failure both haunted and motivated me. At the age of 17, I didn't know much about business, but I knew two things: (1) I wanted my dad to be proud of me, and (2) basically, people want to help other people.

The Core Concept of Delegation:
People Want to Help People

Understanding that core concept turned things around for me. I reached out for help. What I found was that businesspeople are eager to help others (with the possible exception of direct competitors). I asked anyone who would listen how they thought I could save my failing business, and I was inundated with stories of success and best practices. It was one of these practices that helped me turn the corner in my business.

Upon the advice of a mentor, I adjusted my store hours, staying open later than my direct competition. In combination with this, I decided to carry a clothing line that would appeal to the late-night club crowd. It was a relatively simple adjustment, and it worked. I had found a niche and an untapped market. My love for my business led to curiosity, which led to change, which gave me the edge I needed. Within eight years, I had made my first million. Since then, I've been able to turn multiple passions into prosperous businesses and careers. I've been a bestselling music and television producer, author, speaker, and successful entrepreneur, and I've appeared on numerous radio and TV shows across North America. Today one of the things I enjoy most is helping small business owners transform their businesses by showing them how to not only play ball with the big corporations, but also to beat them at their own game.

DO WHAT YOU LOVE — UNTIL YOU BECOME GOOD AT IT

I was able to do what I loved because my parents never told me that I couldn't. But choosing to do what you love isn't necessarily the same as doing what you're good at. If you have to choose one or the other, I say go with what you love, because if you love it, you'll do it often enough to become good at it.

Steve Martin is one of those people who inspires me. You probably think of him as a comedian, but he's also a Renaissance man. He does what he loves, and he's a great example of a person who does what he loves until he becomes good at it. Among his many hobbies is music. About banjo playing he has said, "I was never that great, but a funny thing happens after you've been playing for 40 years; you wake up one morning and you're pretty damn good."

I've spent three decades in business, not because I've hoped it would make me money (although it has), but because I love it. Along the way I made it a priority to learn everything there was to know about marketing. Of course it's changing all the time, but because I loved it, I became a student of marketing. First I loved it; then I learned about it. This innate love and curiosity led to the knowledge that has allowed me to create numerous successful companies over the years.

Maybe you didn't get the message "do what you love," or maybe you got it, but you ignored it. Did you choose your business for the money? For the benefits? It doesn't matter. Any way you slice it, if you don't love what you do, you're doing the wrong thing. It doesn't matter what you're doing.

Hang on a second before you throw up your hands in defeat—no matter what you're doing, you're not stuck. Even if you've been building your business for years, you can always make changes. And you don't necessarily have to close your doors or sell your business to be happy.

Maybe it *is* time to move on, or maybe it's not your job you hate, but the way you *do* your job. Either way, no matter what the reason, you're not the first person to have found yourself in this position.

The days of working for a company for 30 years and retiring with the gold watch and pension are mostly gone. Not so bad.

Today we have more choices. It's not unusual for someone to switch careers a few times because they keep finding things they like better, or even because they become bored by what they're doing. Change is a positive force.

If you're ready to make changes, the first step is to examine whether it's your business you're dissatisfied with or an aspect of your business that's not working. Think of it as a marriage: you might enjoy being married, but discover your spouse's minor idiosyncrasies are worse than bamboo under your fingernails. A good relationship will allow for an open line of communication to resolve issues. You kiss and make up and the next thing you know, you're celebrating 20 years together. The same goes for your business. Chances are if you were to make changes in the way you do things, it would change the way you feel about your work.

Over the next few pages, I'm going to show you how to gain insight into what stands between you and satisfaction with your business. I've provided a series of Power Moves that will help you move in the right direction. As you follow along, it'll be obvious whether it's time to walk down a new street. Is it time to find a new business or fix what's not working with the one you have? Your level of satisfaction may simply be a matter of finding the right kind of help.

THE RIGHT KIND OF HELP

One of the things I wasn't always good at was finding the right kind of help. But because I love business, over the years I've become better and better at identifying the kind of help I need. I've been able to surround myself with people who are not only the most successful at what they do, but who sincerely care about the quality of their products and services. I've learned to understand the intricacies of delegation: which tasks can be delegated, how, and to whom. And I've learned that delegation doesn't always involve human beings.

With the rise in online marketing and social media, support services are popping up for every imaginable task. Blogging networks, social media, and aggregation software are all available to work for us—even on weekends and holidays.

> ## POWER MOVE
> Surround yourself with successful people.

THE OUTSOURCING PARADIGM

1

VIRTUAL ASSISTANT

Most people either don't enjoy administrative tasks or don't have time to perform them well. What happens is one of two things: quality work is compromised when they tackle (or avoid) the work, or they pay exorbitant fees by schlepping their administrative projects to major retail office-support stores. In either case, profit is directly affected by expenses or lost customers.

Outsourcing to a competent virtual assistant (VA) will not only save time and money but also help to ensure you don't lose clients because of substandard administrative practices. A VA is an independent professional who remotely provides administrative support services for numerous clients in a multiplicity of industries. In addition to administrative services such as telephone support, e-mail management, organization, and so forth, they also serve clients in creative and technical capacities.

Obviously they don't work for free, so how does a virtual assistant save you money? I love this question. There are a few things you may be taking for granted in operating your business, expenses you really didn't think about. For instance, take office space and office equipment. If you have an administrative person on staff, at the very least you'll need to provide a desk, a chair, a computer, and a printer—and of course a place for them to sit and file their nails. Oh, and don't forget about the water cooler for wasted time spent chatting on breaks, and a phone for personal calls.

Have you priced office space lately? Depending on what part of the country you're in and what side of town, it can be pretty costly. How about computers and computer programs? Software and computer applications cost a small fortune, and once your business begins to grow, you can't afford not to invest in technology for your in-house employee(s). It's starting to come together now, isn't it?

A VA works from home or from another remote location, so other than software or applications specific to your business, you won't need to worry about providing any of these things. Price them out and then calculate the savings. The truth is, if you're outsourcing to a VA, you may not even need an Internet connection!

So, is the idea of outsourcing to a VA becoming more appealing? It gets better when you consider that your business could enjoy the benefits of highly skilled professionals performing tasks—some of which, if you were to do them yourself, would find you struggling to reach the level of mediocrity. Along with VAs who provide basic administrative support, there are those who specialize in specific areas. Skilled writers can produce expert newsletters, create documents, and contribute to other projects. A tech-savvy VA can design your blog or website, perform social media functions, and help with your Internet marketing. Once you find the right person to outsource your tasks to, the synergy between you will affect your business in positive ways. You'll be free to work *on* your business instead of *in* it, and your success potential can shoot right through the roof.

GLOBALIZING DELEGATION

As business becomes more global, delegation is more important than ever. In such a mega-competitive environment, our first instinct is to dig in and hunker down, but survival depends on doing just the opposite: reaching out. Yes, the world is a smaller place, and we now have access as never before to brick and mortar businesses as well as online companies in many parts of the world. Our workload has also increased because of this. In order to excel, every entrepreneur must know what, why, when, and how to delegate—and that's exactly what this book is all about.

Today I know a few more things about business than I did when I stood in that empty store in Hollywood, but a couple of things haven't changed. I still want to make my dad proud (although now he's looking on from the Great Beyond), and I'm still confident that the most important business skill is knowing when and where to get help—that is, how to harness the power of delegation.

Daily Tasks versus Income-Generating Activities

Let's do an experiment. Take a blank sheet of paper and draw a line down the middle. In the left-hand column, list your "tasks," such as responding to e-mail. On the right-hand side, list "income-generating activities" (IGAs), those actions that result in immediate income to your business.

Look at your lists. If you're like most people, your tasks column includes activities such as returning phone calls, dealing with e-mail (including deleting spam), planning, research, Internet marketing, accounting, invoicing, paying bills, meetings, sales calls, writing copy, and bookkeeping.

Now, transfer from the tasks to the IGA column those daily tasks that, though simple, you might choose to do because you enjoy them or because you're convinced you can do them better, faster, and cheaper than anyone else.

If You Want Something Done Right—Delegate It!

Look at the items remaining in your tasks column. While these tasks may be necessary, are they really building your business? Here's another question: Could any of these tasks be delegated? Set aside for a moment your belief in the adage "If you want something done right, do it yourself," and put check marks beside those items on your list that could be performed by a competent individual with some training (and initial supervision) by you or a member of your staff. Most likely, you've checked nearly every one of your tasks.

But what about your IGAs? How many of those could be delegated? Some, most likely. Place check marks beside those items. Those items left unchecked comprise what you should be doing in a day. That list probably includes "big-ticket" items such as brainstorming new products or services or developing business relationships.

This is what Steven Covey meant when he distinguished between *important* versus *urgent* activities. How many of your income-generating activities are not getting done while you focus on urgent (but not important) daily tasks? How much more productive, profit-generating, and enjoyable would your day be if you focused only on your IGAs?

By the way, your desire to work less doesn't mean you're lazy. If you're wondering how worthiness and hard work became intertwined in the first place, it stems from an old concept called, "the Protestant work ethic," a belief that hard work and frugality were important qualities of the righteous. It was something people strove for, and when they believed they fell short, it affected their self-image and sense of worthiness. Along with various other antiquated concepts, it's been handed down through the generations, and a lot of people are subliminally influenced by it. Human culture rewards self-sacrifice. Suffering is revered. If you're not paying attention, you'll get caught up in this mind-set. It won't move you forward. All it will do is create inner conflict as you try to move away from it.

So, let's get this straight before we go any further: there's absolutely nothing wrong with your desire to work less, your desire to be rich, or your desire to shift responsibility to someone else. When you believe this at a core level, you'll free yourself to benefit fully from outsourcing and ultimately achieving boundless quality of life.

PRODUCTIVITY VERSUS BUSYNESS

A common misconception of those in the rat race is that when they're busy, they're being productive. Not true. Unless you're paying close attention to what you're doing, busyness can keep you from being productive. It all depends on what you're busy doing.

A client of mine noticed that the number of people she knew began to increase when she joined Facebook in 2007. She thought that the more time she spent on Facebook, the more relationships she'd build. True, to a certain extent. She joined groups, commented on interesting posts, and chatted with her new friends. It didn't take long, however, for her to realize that she was spending more time maintaining relationships than she was working her business. She soon became overwhelmed by her social media tasks. She was so caught up, she wasn't sure how to break free.

By analyzing her productivity and implementing a time management plan, she was able to bring things back into perspective. She began outsourcing many of her social media tasks to a VA, who actually implemented a successful social media marketing campaign. By doing so, my client discovered she had freed up three hours a day. Until she outsourced a few tasks, she had been busy but not productive.

We can define productivity in several ways, but at its most basic level, it can be seen as creating the most value in the least amount of time. Productivity can be distinguished from busyness in that busyness refers more to the consumption of time by activity. If you're going to understand the difference in your business, it's important to recognize the line that separates these two concepts. You can make yourself busy doing just about anything—surfing the Net, volunteering for committees, or, for that matter, baking cookies. You will be productive only if your activities are chosen wisely for the value they provide.

List your tasks and IGAs.

POWER MOVE
*Implement a time management plan
to increase productivity.*

IS THE TIME RIGHT?

Here it comes. This is the card no one would blame you for playing. You can't take action if all your ducks aren't in a row, can you? That wouldn't make good business sense, would it? Not in *this* economy, right?

Can you handle the truth? There will never be a perfect time for anything. You'll always find a reason for choosing not to grab the brass ring unless you admit to yourself that your arms are not too short and there's no time like now to reach out and seize it. Anything less is an excuse, a crutch. Are you still willing to settle for inertia, or are you prepared to move forward?

I get that this is a big step for some people. In fact, it's the point at which some people stop dead, willing to slink back into mediocrity. Why? Because stepping forward means they'll have to give up a little control. That would be like jumping off a cliff. Outsourcing does require you to let go, but remember, if you're prepared, you have a parachute.

How will you know when the time is right to begin outsourcing? Once you're clear about the tasks you want to outsource and what you want to keep for yourself, you're ready to go. Start small or go for it in a big way, aware that you may make mistakes or misjudgments. Everyone does. Ask anyone who's ever tried something new. You can adjust accordingly as you go along. Just step forward, take a deep breath, and jump. Trust that your parachute will open.

Your Strengths

How do you know what you're best at? This is actually easier to determine than figuring out what you're *not* so good at (unless you're on a bowling team and you keep throwing gutter balls, in which case you should take the hint and switch to Ping-Pong). You may know some of your weaknesses and may be in denial about others. If you think carefully, life has probably tipped you off more than once. Maybe you just weren't paying attention.

> ### POWER MOVE
> *Pay attention.*

None of us is good at everything. The sooner you accept this fact, the easier it'll be for you to hand off the stuff someone else could do better. Go ahead and spend a lot of time in therapy if you want, or just come to terms with it now. Once you do, you'll be one step closer to increasing your productivity through outsourcing.

Successful Delegation

Once you've divided the tasks specific to running your business from your income-generating activities (IGAs), your task list will give you information about what you can delegate. Whether you're a lone wolf or you manage a large staff, there are going to be tasks that only you can or want to perform, perhaps those that define you as a businessperson. But there may be smaller tasks associated with your IGAs that you can delegate. For instance, if you're a graphic designer, you may not want to delegate artwork to someone else. But you may be able to delegate a search for font styles or clip art. If you work as a writer, you've earned your reputation because you write well. You can, however, delegate proofreading and copyediting to someone you've trained. As long as you feel comfortable doing so, flip things like that over to the task list.

WHAT EXACTLY IS OUTSOURCING?

If you understand delegating, you'll understand outsourcing. The difference: delegating is the process of assigning a task to someone who may or may not require compensation. It's kind of like parents assigning a list of chores to their kids: sometimes they get an allowance for their "hard labor" (outsourcing), and other times they don't (delegation).

Outsourcing is attached to compensation. It's the process of paying someone else to do what either you or an employee *could do* but that would be done more efficiently or with less cost by someone else. Before outsourcing became a popular means of doing business, companies were forced to hire new employees every time they had a need, no matter how large or small the job. As employees, those people continued to be paid whether or not there was a task to perform.

The term *outsourcing* became very popular in the 90s following the Internet boom. New companies were not large enough to handle the demands of operating in a global economy. Internet marketers and high tech companies began outsourcing projects to experts in the field to avoid having to hire new employees. The first jobs widely outsourced before the turn of the new century were in customer service. High tech companies hired people to answer incoming calls from customers requiring tech support. Regardless of how many employees you have, there is always a place for outsourcing within your company. Even if you're just starting a business, this book will show you why outsourcing can be important to the success of your business and how to manage it efficiently.

Understood as the management or completion of a function by a third party vendor or service provider, outsourcing is often referred to as subcontracting. It's really not a new concept. People have been outsourcing for generations. Do you hire a gardener? How about a housekeeper once a week? Both are great examples of outsourcing. You could pull your own weeds or clean your own toilet, but either you prefer not to do it, or you know someone else can do a better job, so you outsource the work.

Businesses often outsource payroll. Tax preparation, bookkeeping, and business plans are also typically outsourced to individuals more qualified for the job. Just ask anyone who's done their own taxes and been audited by the IRS. In many cases, if they'd only used a CPA, they may not have found themselves on the federal chopping block. Outsourcing can pay for itself. Professional tax preparers may find ways to decrease your tax bill and more than cover their expense by securing a refund.

Speaking of payroll, once you master outsourcing, you may find you don't even need payroll. You'll probably find there's an independent contractor for every task. Not only will this reduce your operating expenses (no workers' comp, no SSI, no benefits), but outsourcing will also offer more flexible payment arrangements. We'll talk a little more about this later.

Whether you're delegating to an employee or outsourcing to a vendor, you'll be able to work faster and easier, and your business will be more profitable. Today, you can build your business with nothing more than your cell phone and laptop. Most importantly, you'll save time.

Take a look at how Anushka Drescher outsourced a newsletter and not only saved money but padded her pockets at the same time:

> Two weeks ago, I started outsourcing. I got a wonderful assistant named Maria, and she has helped me so much already. She helped build a database of customers. She also created a mind map for my whole business. All of the things that I need to do, she puts them on a visual map online. I take my electronic notes every day, I highlight the parts that are action items, I e-mail her my notes, and she creates another visual mind map of all the actions I need to take. When I get home, I know exactly what I need to do.
>
> Maria has been amazing, she's always ready to please, she's always friendly, and she's always helpful. I am just so grateful that I came across her. She's going to save me a lot of time and money. She's going to be preparing a newsletter that I get paid $500 to do once a month. It'll take her about two hours once I train her, and it will pay for her entire month's salary.

Anushka increased her company's profits by outsourcing her newsletter to a VA. She also used her VA's services for the rest of the month with nothing more out of pocket.

HOW TO BEGIN OUTSOURCING

So you've decided to outsource. Where do you begin? Good question. Start by reviewing your task list. Which would be the easiest tasks to outsource? That's a great place to start. As you begin to trust and let go, move over to your IGA list. When I first began outsourcing, I noticed as I became more comfortable with delegating, my IGA list got shorter. This will happen when you find and train the right people. That sets the great disappearing act into motion.

Just as it's easier to keep existing clients than it is to prospect for new ones, it's easier to keep working with the same service providers. Over time, they'll get to know you and the way you like things done, and there's nothing better than working with people who know you almost as well as you know yourself. In order to do it better, you'd have to hire your mother—which might not be a bad idea. You'd probably get lunch, too.

How do you hire and retain the right support team? If you make the effort from the beginning, you'll save money and needless aggravation. First, it's important to determine what you're looking for. What are your goals and objectives? Ask yourself a few questions so you'll know the best place to begin your search for the best kind of support:

1. What am I looking for in a provider? Familiarizing yourself with the tasks you plan to outsource will help answer this question.

2. How will I know when I've met the right person(s)? What characteristics are you looking for? Specific skills?

3. How will I evaluate whether I'm on the right track with a project? (We'll talk more about how to do this.)

Once you've prioritized your task list and determined which tasks you're planning to outsource first, these questions will be easier to answer. Go to your task list and rewrite it, placing the most important tasks at the top and working down. Begin with the highest-priority task.

Knowing what you're looking for in a provider before you begin your search is important. The first person you hire may become vital to the success of your business and be able to handle several or even all of the items on your task list. As the title of this book says, *outsource smart*. Take your time and be thorough. The person you hire will be the first to support you in living the laptop lifestyle.

Interview Multiple People

If you've answered the first two questions in the list above, you now know who you're looking for, and you know how you'll know you've found that person. It may be a specific skill set, geographical location, or personality type. Whatever it is, the criteria you establish will aid you in your search. Remember Amanda, the mother played by Sally Field in *Mrs. Doubtfire*? She knew exactly what she wanted from a housekeeper/nanny. As her estranged husband, Daniel, played by Robin Williams, impersonated several characters, one by one she crossed them off the list—until Mrs. Doubtfire (also played by Robin Williams) called. "She" more than met the criteria, and after a short qualifying interview, Amanda hired "her" on the spot.

Your first step: knowing what you want and interviewing—either remotely or in person—those who meet your criteria.

Keep in mind, even if they pass the first qualifier, not every person will work out to your expectations. Everyone works differently, and we all have different performance standards. There are people whose values match your own. Those are the people you want to find, but you may not know they're a match until you give them the opportunity to perform.

Test Those Who Pass "Inspection"

The way to know if a provider is right for your business is to give those who pass inspection an opportunity to prove themselves with a small project. Make sure the project is not one that would affect your business if results aren't up to par. If you're happy with the quality of the work and the person fits your other criteria, he/she might be a great fit for your business.

You might think that because your business is small—a sole proprietorship or a home-based business—delegating isn't necessary. To the contrary! With the growing popularity home businesses have achieved in recent years, outsourcing and delegating have likewise become immensely popular. People who want to take their businesses in a new direction rely on outsourcing and look for capable people to collaborate and team with.

If there weren't considerable benefits involved, outsourcing wouldn't have become as popular as it is today. In lieu of bringing on more employees, large corporations have begun outsourcing major areas of their work to global professionals. They're saving billions of dollars. In fact, let's take a minute and talk specifically about outsourcing as it relates to big business.

Outsourcing for Medium to Large Companies

If you own or manage a business with more than a few employees, you're probably already delegating within your organization, but there are many ways you can expand on this to increase efficiency and hang onto a few greenbacks. Companies that outsource projects to independent contractors or firms will find many benefits associated with doing so. Depending on the nature of business and whether there's a need for hands-on production or projects that can be completed remotely, outsourcing processes and contractors vary. If you have a project or assignment your employees can't handle, hiring a contractor to assist you can have more than one advantage. Mike Crow, a business coach, shares his experience with outsourcing and how it impacted his employees:

> I coach other coaches who are trying to create their own next programs. Currently I'm outsourcing to a VA, a young lady by the name of Sheila, and she just does an incredible job. She's helping us with list building, she's helping us set meet-up groups, and she's helping us reinforce continuity of our information on the Internet. I have 10 people here who work for me. I didn't hire the virtual assistant for *me*; I hired her for my top two people. I was thinking about letting her go, but my employees almost quit on me. They said, "If you do that, we gotta do all her work, and we don't wanna do that." So you know what? She ain't goin' anywhere anytime soon.

Mike found a way to support his existing staff without having to hire another employee. His VA became indispensable to his business.

Outsourcing to another vendor or VA means you won't have to bring on another employee for a project that may be temporary. By avoiding having to add that new employee to your payroll, outsourcing allows you to save money on employee benefits, which can cut deeply into your profits over time. When you outsource a project, you can kiss those expenses good-bye. You'll never have to worry about insurance, workers' comp, or contributing to 401Ks because the person you are hiring will be an independent contractor. You'll cut them a check or make a PayPal payment at the end of a pay period, and that will be that. No deductions, no taxes—definitely a more cost efficient method of doing business. And if someone doesn't work out the way you'd hoped, you can discontinue the relationship and move on to another provider.

Gain Knowledge

In addition to saving you money, outsourcing offers other benefits. As you begin to outsource, you'll interface with industry professionals with different skill sets, an opportunity to gain knowledge and expertise in new areas.

As you'll see throughout this book, using contractors or VAs with special skills not only can save money, it can help you make money. With access to a pool of skilled professionals, you may be able to take on projects you would otherwise have to turn away. You can hire an outside vendor to complete the job, and as Internet marketer Mike Evans discovered, you may come away with a little learning and training yourself:

> I just want to share how much I enjoy outsourcing to VAs. The reason is, they make me money. I have a full-time assistant in the Philippines who works the same hours I do. He comes at noon my time and leaves at 9 p.m. my time, which is good for me because I get up at 10 a.m. and start working around noon. Now that I've trained him, he is able to come up with ideas on his own to help me make money. I'm in a very complicated business, Internet marketing. A lot of things have to be in perfect order for me to make money. He never makes a mistake, except when I give him the wrong information. He's also able to take initiative and make decisions on his own. He offers suggestions to help me make more money. A lot of times, he thinks of things to do that I haven't taught him. That's the biggest value I'm getting from my personal assistant.

If, as Mike did, you can hook up with a VA who's invested enough in your success that he is willing to offer suggestions that make you money, you've hit the mother lode. As I said earlier, if you want to have the most successful experience with outsourcing, it's advantageous to search for the most qualified provider for your particular project and spend some time in training. Carefully choosing the provider will ensure you end up with a quality result.

Human Resources Gets a Break

When a new employee is hired into a medium or large business, the human resources department spends a lot of time and effort preparing files and setting up the new employee with benefits, payroll, etc. By outsourcing, you'll free your human resources department to concentrate on more important aspects of the company. When you outsource, human resources doesn't even get involved. That in itself saves time and money.

Flexibility

Outsourcing will offer your company a great range of flexibility. Since you never have to hire the VA or contractor directly, you'll be able to work with her on an intermittent basis. This is helpful when you have a project that pops up out of nowhere and you need immediate assistance.

Whether you own the world's largest manufacturer of mechanical bulls, or you hawk goods from a wooden cart on the sidewalk, outsourcing will affect your quality of life in ways you may not have expected. You may think the life of your dreams is miles down the road, but it doesn't have to be. Because they've learned to outsource smart, these guys have found a way to have it all:

Blake Goodwin

Many people have been asking me, "Blake, how do you get it all done? How do you get so much done so fast? We're seeing the amount of work that you keep putting out. I constantly see you on Facebook, on Twitter, on MySpace, on YouTube; you're out there in all the social networks."

The answer is, I have a secret weapon in my back pocket: my VA. I've been outsourcing for a long time, and it's allowed me to go to the gym, to go to the golf course, to spend time with my wife and my family. It's also allowed me to get into a real comfortable position knowing that everything is going to be taken care of behind the scenes. People are always contacting me and saying, "Blake, I just saw your new post on Facebook" and I'm like, "I haven't even logged in to Facebook in six months."

I like to share all my secret weapons and strategies. Outsourcing is one that will definitely skyrocket you to the next level.

Justin Tillman

Being a young entrepreneur, you kind of focus on the little tasks as well as the big tasks. You've got only 24 hours in a day. I now have a virtual assistant who works with me. She's able to take care of some tasks that might have taken up a whole day of my time, which would have had me working all weekend. Now, I can spend that time with my family, and I really enjoy my weekends.

Maybe you've been running yourself ragged for so long you don't remember what it was like to value your time. Pick something on your task list and outsource just one task. See what a difference it makes.

VALUING YOUR TIME

There are tons of gurus out there trying to sell you the latest, greatest "key to success," but I truly believe that the key to success is what it always has been: valuing your time. Amid all of the technological advances, that core truth has not changed. What must change is how we use our time.

How do we figure out our time value? We take our annual income and divide it by the number of hours we work. Correct? Yes, this is correct, but can you go out and buy more time? No. Can Martha Stewart? Can Bill Gates? No. Time is priceless. So start treating it like it's priceless. You have to get some of that precious time back, because there's only so much of it, and you can't buy more. Why delegate? Simply put, is your time worth more than $6 per hour? I hope the answer to that question is "yes." But if you're working 16 hours a day, you're acting as if the answer is "no." If your time is worth more than $6 an hour, you should be outsourcing or delegating anything below your pay grade.

In any business, there are tasks that are redundant, that are mindless, or that require some expertise but don't have to be done by the principal. That is true of every single business. All of those redundant tasks that can be done by someone at a lower pay grade should be delegated or outsourced to someone else. It should be done—and it is being done—by your competitors. It's not a new principle, only a new playing field.

Do What You Like

I'm constantly being asked, "What are the tasks that I should keep for myself?" As a general rule, I say: keep what you *like* to do. That's the whole point. You can outsource just about everything—graphic work, data entry, secretarial services, transcription, and e-mail—but by all means, if you enjoy a task, do it yourself.

DELEGATION REDEFINED

The path to outsourcing smart and living the laptop lifestyle is through delegation. But wait! Forget the image of a secretary sitting across a desk from her boss while she takes dictation. We need a new definition of delegation—one that works for the twenty-first century.

Delegation has changed dramatically in response to a globalized economy and world-connecting technologies. Many of us no longer delegate to an administrative assistant in our office but to a virtual assistant a half a world way. (Even local errands, such as picking up copy center orders, are now often done via courier service.) We also delegate to a nonhuman helper: the Internet. The purpose of this book is to show you how this new kind of delegation will revolutionize your business and free you to live the life of your dreams. It may sound clichéd or too good to be true, but I'm doing it, so I know you can, too.

Designing/Maintaining Your Website

It used to be you had to outsource everything Web, unless you were familiar with HTML. Most people are not. It's a language reserved for professionals, and as consumers we pay dearly for their services. Now, thanks to WordPress, everyday people can not only design their own websites, but they can also maintain them. Good news? In most cases, no.

Nevermind that WordPress technology has made it simple to create your own website or blog. For the same reasons you hire a doctor when you're sick and a lawyer if you have legal issues, unless you're a skilled designer, you should outsource your website. Surf the Web any day and you'll find all sorts of websites. Though you may not be able to tell a $5,000 site from one that cost (choke) $20,000, the ones made by amateurs will surely stand out. I'm telling you, you won't miss them. You have anywhere from 30 seconds to a minute to hold someone's attention when they click onto your site. Unless you want to risk losing potential customers, be sure you take this aspect of your business seriously. It's easier to engage a new client by making a good first impression than it is to change her mind after she's already formed an opinion.

A VA specializing in web design (and some of them do know HTML, too) will have a better chance at creating a website that will not only pique visitors' interest but also keep their attention long enough for them to get to know what you're all about. Hopefully they'll be prompted to contact you for information. The difference between outsourcing to a tech-savvy VA and hiring a conventional web designer is this: because they work with you on several levels, your VA knows *you*. He understands your business and is familiar with your goals. In a way, your VA steps into your skin. Once you develop a sound working relationship, outsourcing your web related projects to a VA can be almost like doing the work yourself—*without* the effort.

Many VAs understand the technology to install shopping carts, member applications, and other features on your website. Even if you're using WordPress, you can outsource maintenance, updates, and—unless you really want to keep it for yourself—your blog.

Doing Your Own Blogging

Blogging is increasingly being used by businesspeople to market, brand, and build databases. A blog is an online forum where you disseminate information or communicate a message to customers and prospects. Every business has a specific way it wants its message conveyed, so blogging is an area that many businesspeople don't like to delegate. Fair enough. You can do your own blogging if you have an important message you feel only you can convey, or even if you enjoy writing. But remember the trade-off. The more tasks you keep, the more of that overwhelmed feeling you keep.

What if I told you most business blogs are not read word-for-word? What if I told you most are not even skimmed? Would that change your ideas about the necessity of doing it yourself? Maybe a list of critical points and a competent person to delegate the task to would work just as well. How much of your time would that free, and how could you use that extra time to move your business forward?

Blogging as Marketing

If you decide to outsource your blog, and if your knowledge of keywords and Google ranking is limited, you'll want to find a professional who either has the facts or can be trained to incorporate specific elements into your blogs. Why? Because if you want to compete on a global (or even local) level, you'll need decent search-engine rankings. Rankings can make or break your business. Google, as an Internet search engine, assigns a value to each element of a website with the purpose of measuring its relative importance. If you're in business for the long haul and you want to take advantage of Internet marketing to grow your business, this is not something to leave to chance.

Visit the site of just about any business and you'll probably find a blog. Maybe two. Depending on the size of the company, multiple blogs might be used for a variety of reasons. You can bet one of them is marketing.

Not only are blogs growing in popularity as one of the hottest forms of digital media, but as many of us are discovering, they can be an effective way to build relationships with customers at a time when antiquated marketing methods seem impersonal. The best way to foster intimacy with your audience is to find the place where rapport and authentic concern intersect. When done correctly, a blog can accomplish this.

If you want to write your own blog, there are resources for learning how to create one. Know that a blog is more than just a collection of words and, if done properly, will help you achieve desired results. If you make mistakes, it can do just the opposite. A word of caution: if you know what you'd like to say but write poorly, you can sabotage the very thing that's meant to connect you with your audience. Using poor grammar or the wrong words will crush your credibility. On the other hand, if you write well but have a hidden agenda, your readers will see right through you. They'll hear what you're "not saying."

Worse yet, if you make your agenda obvious and your readers feel used or manipulated, they'll stop visiting your blog. Once you've alienated them, most will never come back. Is this something you want to risk? If not, outsourcing to a qualified support person might be another item for your task list.

The number one rule of thumb when it comes to blogs is this: make sure your blog is an authentic conversation between you and your audience. A blog is a virtual community, and your readers need to perceive value if they're going to commit their time to reading it. Likewise, to qualify as authentic, your blog must accurately reflect your values and the image of your business. If you already have a blog, go back and look at it. How are you doing?

Blogs that come off as transparent marketing pieces and are saturated with ad copy or promotional messages are bound for a certain outcome: failure. Your prospects will fall away like leaves from a tree after an autumn frost. Remember, they're busy too. Unless they're getting valuable or interesting information, they'll probably not waste their time.

Of course, your blog should promote your products and services. That's the reason for blogging in the first place. When done well, your blog can market and grow your business like nothing else. Did you see the movie *Julie & Julia*? The author of that blog was an "average Jane" who became a multimillionaire by garnering a following so large that Hollywood based a movie on her book, which was based on her blog. How did she do it? She was authentic, respectful, and clear with her intentions. Handle that and you've handled more than uneducated bloggers who bury their businesses, digging deeper with every word.

> ## POWER MOVE
> Understand Google-ranking and keywords
> or find someone who does.

Blogging as Search Optimization

Today, many small businesses use blogging as a search engine optimization tool. Search engine optimization (SEO) is the process of organically directing traffic to your website or blog. It's free. All major search engines, such as Google, Yahoo, and Bing, rank web pages, videos, and other content based on what the search engine considers most relevant to users.

By creating numerous, frequent (even imperfect) blogs, you create the perception that you're current, active, and an industry leader—at least that's how the search engines will interpret it. So you'll want to have many pages with your company information out there for the search engines to find.

As I said earlier, you can create those many pages of blog content yourself, or you can have a VA do it. If you know that you're most effective and generate the most income for your company by orchestrating from the top, I suggest delegating your blogging to VAs—but not just any VAs.

Delegating Your Blogging

It goes without saying that you need to delegate writing to a VA who is fluent in English. You also want to find someone whose voice is as close to your own as possible. One of my associates hired a VA, James, to write one of his blogs. He wanted James to get a feel for his conversational style, so he sent him recordings. He spoke into his iPod as he traveled so James could get a feel for who he was.

Today, James writes in my associate's voice for one of his blogs. My associate writes articles periodically for that blog himself, and when he looks back on the posts, he tells me it's impossible for him to discern which ones were written by James and which were written by him. So much for the importance of doing it all yourself!

The point is, as long as the ideas being conveyed are yours, and as long as your blog is meeting the criteria outlined earlier, you should have no qualms about delegating this task as you would any other. Hire a freelancer to do your blogs, or use a managed facility (many managed facilities have teams of American writers to write blog content). The important thing is, if it's not something you enjoy doing, get it off your plate. Once you do, you'll be one step closer to living the lifestyle of your dreams.

WHAT SHOULD NOT BE DELEGATED: STRATEGIC PLANNING

There are some things I do not outsource or delegate. I don't outsource the writing of books to VAs (although there are some who could do it), and I don't outsource the actual planning of my business. I have many people who assist me in strategic planning, but a VA doesn't have my experience, so I keep most of that for myself. A VA may perform strategic steps but not the actual strategic planning.

The real answer to the question "What should never be delegated?" is "Never say never." I'm constantly amazed at how much and how quickly my VAs learn; their level of expertise seems to grow exponentially. In short, there's very little you can't outsource. The key is in training and systems.

OUTSOURCING
EVENT MANAGEMENT

Throwing events has been a huge marketing channel for our company and can be a huge marketing channel for your company as well. There are so many kinds of events that, as host, you can benefit from. Some are live, such as seminars, boot camps, symposia, meet-up groups, networking meetings, business mixers, training programs, and so forth. And some are virtual, such as webinars, teleseminars, and video conferencing—all popular ways of connecting with remote audiences.

If you can't handle the task in-house, event planners can be hired. That's definitely a great form of outsourcing, but it can cost you your first born, depending on how complex the event is. On average, most qualified event planners charge a fee of between 15 and 20 percent of the total cost of an event. Hourly fees are usually between $75 and $100, depending on the complexity of the event and amount of time required to plan and execute it. Working with a VA or team of VAs can be much more practical, not to mention economical.

There are a few things you won't be able to outsource. One of those is reading this book, so if you were starting to get ideas, forget about it. We talked about strategic planning earlier. With the high cost of producing events, that's not something you want to outsource. You know your business better than anyone else. Your event is a reflection on and extension of your brand. Understanding your industry in terms of needs and wants, knowing the buying habits of your niche market, and having an end goal in mind will provide a platform for launching your event.

Based on the type of event you're hosting, determine the outsourcing component, and, with a little salt and pepper, you'll produce a pretty tasty event. Here are a few things to consider as you prepare your task list for outsourcing:

Type of event. Are you hosting a live event or virtual? What's the time frame? The date? Do you have a specific location in mind?

Mission. Define the purpose of your event. Doing so will help you target your efforts. Why are you bringing people together? Are you using this event to build your database? Market a future event?

Audience/guests. Who are you inviting—anyone who will pay, or will you pre-qualify? Will your guest list consist primarily of existing clients or newly acquired prospects?

Marketing. Where will you promote your event? Will you use affiliates to help circulate the information, or is this a private function?

Cost. What expenses will be associated with the event: advertising, space rental, staffing, materials, production, audio/visual equipment, etc.?

When you've fleshed out your event, you'll have the big picture, and you'll be able to create a task list. Some of the tasks you'll keep for yourself, but remember, the more you assign to someone else, the better. Keep only those tasks you enjoy or can't outsource effectively.

Although there are so many more tasks that fall between the lines, below is an example of opportunities to outsource responsibilities for a live event. Virtual events will be a little easier but, as anyone who's worked behind the scenes will say, not quite as easy as they seem. In fact, if your team members are doing their jobs, guests will have no idea how much is being attended to virtually.

Sample Task List for a Live Event

Arrangements. Facility rental, production, paperwork, price-shopping, ordering materials, printing, hospitality, booking hotel rooms, transportation, hunting for sponsors, contacting vendors, hiring performers, and securing speakers.

Research. Media sources, speaker options, products and services, support materials, guest blogging opportunities, and securing inbound links from related sites.

Communication. Telephone calls and e-mails to participants and speakers/staff, reminders, speaker bios, designing press packets, securing a conference line, and sending the number to attendees. Be sure your VA speaks excellent English.

Promotion. Social media status updates, event posting and replies, comments in niche groups, setting up radio and TV interviews, mailing lists, and press releases.

Collateral design. Invitations, flyers, tickets, order forms, image release forms, questionnaires, ad copy, and speaker agreements.

Onsite production. Seating, staging, audio-visual setup, sales table, speakers table, timeline, program schedule, signage, meal breaks, parking, managing logistics, and implementation.

Onsite management. Staff and volunteer supervision, and direction for outsourced personnel (e.g., photographer, videographer, caterer).

After event. Sales reports, communication with purchasers, sending speakers' payments, handling returns and cancelations, packing and shipping materials back to office or storage, ordering and replenishing stock, thank-you cards and phone calls, reviewing and paying hotel bill and other open invoices.

. . . and don't forget about the after-party!

Whew! If you're not inspired to outsource after this, I suggest you call someone who's tried to do it all for herself and get her feedback—if she's still doing events.

PROJECT MANAGEMENT

A project is a fully self-contained, temporary venture designed to meet a specific goal. It's usually defined by a beginning and an end. You can look at it as a complex series of tasks meant to bring about positive change or add value to an existing situation.

Project management involves planning, organizing, and managing objectives like materials, budget, and the skilled people who will contribute to achieve the goal of the project. As an entrepreneur with a growing business, you no doubt have many projects going at the same time. If you're going to ensure you maintain quality production and exemplary service, outsourcing will have tremendous value for you.

Depending on what you have going on, you can manage your own projects and outsource specific tasks, or you can outsource whole projects to a managing VA you trust to follow through. The longer you work with service providers or individuals, the easier it'll be to trust them.

Globalization is changing the way we do business, and change can be a good thing. Today you can almost reach out and touch prospects in other countries. With the right marketing plan in place, you can set up shop just about anywhere. This cuts both ways. Businesses are reaching across the ocean to our shores, too. Turning stumbling blocks into stepping stones, outsourcing is expanding opportunities for all of us.

CHANGE AS FREEDOM

Once you understand the possibilities that come with twenty-first-century delegation, you'll begin to see globalization not as the threat of competition from abroad but as enabling access to profit-boosting outsourcing. Technology will no longer be the scary thing only your neighbor's fourth-grader understands but a tool for lightning-fast business marketing.

Change can be intimidating, but as you read on, you'll see your old fears as new advantages. While your competitors remain too paralyzed by fear of technology and stereotypes about out-sourcing to play the game, you—with the help of tools found in these pages—will not only win the game but win your freedom as well.

OUTSOURCE SCHEDULING

Speaking of freedom, let's start with your mind. Do you calendar your appointments or go by memory? I hope it's the former. The last thing you need is to leave someone sipping iced tea waiting for you while you're at home crunching on a bowl of chips and watching American Idol.

Have you ever missed an exciting teleseminar because you thought you'd remember to call in at 6 p.m.? You can't commit everything to memory. Even if you remember most things most of the time, it'll be the one thing you forget that nails you. Cal-endaring important dates is critical for several reasons, and it only makes sense to peel things off your brain and commit them to paper. Scheduling is easy to outsource, and it'll give you peace of mind.

If you're the kind of person who is hyper-organized, who is super responsible with appointments and is always on time, outsourcing your schedule might be a boundary you can't see crossing. Google Calendar will help put you at ease. It's collaboration-friendly so you can easily share scheduling respon-sibilities with your VA. You'll both know what's going on when, and if you like color coding, you'll love it. Google Calendar is free.

Also, Google Calendar syncs with Outlook if you need it to. Your VA can create several calendars on your account and manage them separately or merge them. There is a task list, and you can view multiple time zones, so if you're working with people around the world, you won't miscalculate and accidentally call them at 2 a.m. Every morning, you'll find your day's agenda in your inbox. This is a great tool for time management.

For a traffic-generating, business building outsourcing tip, go to http://123Employee. com/outsourcesmart/interview/01 or scan this QR code and watch this video now.

THE NEW DEFINITION
OF INSANITY

2

B efore we talk about training and using outsourced VAs, let's talk about fears. One of your fears may involve the process of outsourcing abroad. You may associate the term *outsourcing abroad* with the Kathy Lee Gifford or Nike scandals of the nineties. You may even imagine starving children chained to sewing machines and dingy, Third World working conditions. If so, put those ideas aside. That's not what I'm talking about when I suggest the use of outsourced assistants. One major difference is the industry. We're not talking about manufacturing; we're talking technology. It's a world away (pardon the pun).

OUTSOURCING TODAY:
A WHOLE NEW BALLGAME

The types of tasks you'll be outsourcing will usually involve some computer expertise and business world savvy; you won't be hiring children, and you won't be delegating any manufacturing work. And you certainly won't be paying miniscule wages or employing people in slum-like conditions. In today's world of outsourced business services, well-paid, trained adults who speak excellent

English and have advanced computer and communication skills work in clean, pleasant, well-run facilities—and enjoy doing it. Today, outsourcing is a whole new ballgame.

Fear of Delegating

A few common fears might interfere with your willingness to delegate responsibilities to a VA. I want to acknowledge that these are big fears. They're the very same fears that can stop you from taking all sorts of action. Facing them head on is the only way through them.

First, there's the fear of the unknown. You don't know what you don't know, and sometimes that can be scary. Some people would rather stagnate than risk. Risking involves the willingness to step into trust.

Hopefully you trust yourself, and because you do, you know what you can expect. But when you've always done everything on your own, you don't know that it's possible to trust someone else to do a good job. Taking a few steps to set up your projects for success and working with a competent, well-trained VA make outsourcing not only possible but desirable.

Another thing that stops people, especially perfectionists, from entrusting tasks to others is the fear of failure. Yeah, I said it was a biggie.

Are you someone who really likes to do things *properly*? That's a nice way of asking if you might be a little, well, you know, hard to please—which is a nice way of saying something else. If you're one of those people who think only they can be effective, and you tend to scrutinize the efforts of others, you might struggle a little at first with outsourcing. By the way, there's a difference between efficiency and effectiveness. Efficiency relates to competence, doing any job well in a reasonable amount of time. Effectiveness is knowing *what the right job is* and then doing it right. If you want to reach your full success potential, it's impossible for you to do everything yourself and do it well.

Closely related to the fear of failure is the fear of success. Many businesspeople have kept themselves down because they fear the ramifications of success. "What if I don't know how to handle success?" "How will I manage my money?" "Maybe it's easier just to keep things where I can deal with them." And the biggest one: "Maybe I'm not *good enough*." Fear of appearing less competent than your associates can cause you to short-circuit your success. No doubt about it, outsourcing can put you on the fast track to success, and if you believe you're not *good enough*, you'll avoid it like the plague.

If you're a person who needs validation in the form of compliments, you might fear you'll compromise credibility by outsourcing some of your tasks. If you believe your value comes from what you produce, not from who you are, you might think outsourcing will detract from your importance, leaving you to feel undeserving of compliments. To that I'd like to respectfully suggest you get over it. You can't take compliments to the bank.

Each of these fears can hold you back. Every one of them has the potential to stunt the growth of your business. And all of them can be overcome.

Adam Kappel of Atomic Apps knows what it's like. At first, he had a hard time letting go of tasks he was good at but didn't have time for:

> I've just recently stepped into outsourcing and am starting to give tasks to a VA. At first, I was a little bit hesitant. It was always a challenge for me to delegate tasks, not really knowing what was going to happen. But I have to say I've completely overcome my outsourcing worries. As soon as I give a task to my VAs, they pick it up quickly, and they get it done. They put it into a system that really works.

It can be really challenging to hand over important tasks when you feel you're the only one who can do them to your standards. But if you take the time to properly train VAs, you may discover they don't miss a beat.

Does the Buck Really Have to Stop Here?

Another common fear that keeps many overworked business owners from delegating is loss of control. If you're an entrepreneur, you're probably used to running the show. You might even credit your success to that very fact. You've always run your business with a hands-on, "the buck stops here" attitude, and it's worked so far. Or has it? Do you find yourself working after-hours and on weekends, with little or no vacation time? Do you feel the constant biting guilt of missing out on family time?

Even if you haven't experienced these problems yet, I'm here to tell you, the belief that nobody but you can run your business will eventually cause you to hit a wall. Maybe your father, mother, or even your business guru was able to "run the whole show" throughout his or her career without hitting a wall, but it's only because the wall hadn't been built yet.

Today's business environment is unique. It's fast-paced and tricky, and planned obsolescence is built into the system. Now more than ever, the entrepreneur is faced with a mandate: keep up with ever-changing technology or watch your competitors overtake you. Integrity, diligence, and marketing ability used to put you ahead of the pack, but today you need all of that and more just to keep up. Today, one individual, no matter how savvy, charismatic, or intelligent, is not enough.

Enter again the trust factor. Learned competency is the key to delegating tasks that will free you to grow your business, live your life, and perhaps even save it. By training someone to deal with the things on your task list, you'll suppress the fear of loss of control and increase your level of confidence. Over time you'll begin to delegate more tasks, more often. When you get to the point where you wake up in the morning thinking about what you're going to have for dinner that night, you'll know you've made it.

THE NEW DEFINITION OF INSANITY

Most entrepreneurs want to do everything themselves. But contemporary technologies have put more work on the entrepreneur's plate than one human being can handle. Automation, social media, and Internet marketing were supposed to make our lives easier (and I'm still waiting for that Jetson's jetpack!). But technology has only made things faster and required new competencies. Contemporary entrepreneurs are working 12- and 14-hour days, and the sacrifice is huge. They're sacrificing their personal lives, their families, and their health. So, to those people who are afraid of delegating, think about what happens if you *don't* delegate.

What's the definition of insanity? It's doing the same thing over and over and expecting a different outcome. Well, in today's business world, you're doing *more* of the same thing over and over and expecting an *even better* outcome. That's the new definition of insanity.

So you've got to get help, but you're not used to trusting others with what you've worked your whole life to build. At stake is not only your profit margin but your reputation, which likewise took years (or decades) to build. You'd rather not risk it all by trusting it to others. But, oh yeah—there's that wall. So how and whom do you trust? The solution is easier than you think: you trust yourself, your ability to select, train, monitor, and manage employees. See, it's *still* about you running the show. The only thing you're giving up is proximity. It's not as risky as you think.

Do you want excuses to stand in your way, or are you ready to face the challenge of stepping into a new way of doing things?

I'm guessing you are. If you weren't ready, you'd have stopped reading a long time ago.

Let's take a look at a few common excuses for not delegating.

Excuse #1: Security Risks

One excuse I've heard from businesspeople who won't accept help is that their business secrets are too important. For years I've travelled all over the world speaking about the virtues of outsourcing. One day, I was speaking in Florida and a man came up to me and said he loved the presentation, but he had questions about security. "Using a VA," he asked, "will my client records be secure? Will my data be protected?"

I said, "Huh? That never really even occurred to me." The fact was, I had been running a huge outsourcing center in the Philippines for years, but I had never had any security breaches.

As important and as critical as your data is to you, it's pretty much worthless to a VA halfway around the world. In a sense, I'd say that your business secrets are actually safer in the hands of an outsourced VA. In your hands, your business data is gold; in their hands, it's just digits and letters, really. As a practical matter, people half a world away would have a hard time exploiting your business information.

You can call me idealistic, but I truly believe there's a culture in the Philippines, where I do most of my outsourcing work, that acts as a kind of moral safeguard. Although there is crime in the Philippines (mostly due to poverty), there's not a lot of violent crime. White collar crime is even rarer. The average Filipino who works in my call center goes to church one to three times per week. Now, I'm not naïve enough to believe that churchgoing is an absolute deterrent to crime, but I do believe there is a high cultural value assigned to trustworthiness in the Philippines. There is also a prestige factor that comes with working for an American employer. My Filipino employees are proud to say they have a

U.S. client, and this pride makes them unlikely to jeopardize that relationship by trying to steal business secrets or exploit the relationship in any way.

What Is Your Exposure?

Look at it this way: what is your most proprietary info? It's probably your credit card information, and this is practically a non-issue because of today's sophisticated encryption systems. When working with outsourced VAs, you can ensure that all they see are the last four digits of your credit card. The same is true of Social Security numbers; you can encrypt those as well. Personally, I give my credit card to my key managers who book flights and set up other types of reservations for me. The reality is: what is your exposure? Let's say your VA turns into the biggest crook in the world overnight. What's your exposure? It's $50—the fee your credit card company charges for removing the fraudulent charges.

For some, delegation requires a huge leap of faith. I think your willingness to delegate has a lot to do with personality type. I tend to trust that if I make a mistake, it can be corrected and that nothing is a disaster. If you live in the "pending disaster" mind-set, it's more difficult to let go. It's also more difficult to become successful.

Entrepreneurs who are most successful tend to make quick decisions. You can get there; you just have to learn to trust your decision making. The best way to gain confidence in your decision making is to take some action and make it work. Are there going to be roadblocks? Yes. Are there going to be obstacles? Absolutely. But that's how you learn to trust.

Excuse #2: The Language Barrier

Will language be a barrier in building a successful relationship with an outsourced VA? The answer depends on where you choose to outsource. I do some web development through India, and I've experienced language issues. The web designer doesn't quite understand what I'm saying, or vice versa. But, like anything else, if you stick with it, the kinks get worked out over time. I've now been working with my Indian employees for so many years that language is rarely an issue. You also have to use common sense about what kinds of tasks to delegate to English language learners. Someone who may not speak perfect English may have superior computer programming skills. In that context, a strong accent has no relevance. For a call-center employee, however, English language skills are crucial.

English in the Philippines

In the Philippines, English is the second language of most natives, but it's a close runner-up to their first language, Tagalog. Everybody in the Philippines speaks English, and they're very Westernized. If you crack a joke, they get it, which I think is the ultimate test of cultural fluency. For voice-based services, using a Filipino VA is a safe option. In fact, recently even Indian companies have been switching to the Philippines for phone-based hiring.

Darius Askaripour of The Innovative Investors uses a VA management company in the Philippines. Here are a few words about his experience:

> Virtual assistants are an integral part of any business. They help bridge the gap of needing help, of getting employees, of training people. The VA company I work with carefully filters employees. The company interviews them and puts them in categories based on what they are good at. That way, if you need a person for social media, or you need a person for pay-per-click, or you need a person for a call center or advertising, mortgage, or whatever the case may be, the company can provide VAs who are already trained in that field. This company employs people in the Philippines. All of the employees speak English perfectly. They are educated, they are professional, they give you reports, they

are accountable, and the best thing is, you can give them the tasks you don't want to worry about. I've got one girl over there, Sunny, she's incredible. She basically does the workload of 15 in-house employees.

Alka Dalal, author of *Creative Genius: Tips to Unleash Yours*, has used VAs for a year and has been very happy with their mastery of the English language:

> The VAs do all of my social networking, my article posting, and so many things that free up my time. That way I can do what I'm good at, such as training leaders in creativity and Internet marketing. I write books, and I network while my VAs do all of the work for me on the back end. They are very easy to deal with, they speak excellent English, they write excellent English, and I am really very happy with them!

Your excuses give you a false sense of security. Address them now, or they're going to keep you stuck right where you are. I don't buy that you want to stay there any more than I believe you'll let your fears hold you back from living a life of freedom.

WHAT'S THE ALTERNATIVE?

Now that we've addressed your excuses, let's get back to most managers' greatest fear: delegation. The reality is, delegation is not merely a convenience; it's absolutely necessary to grow your business in today's complicated world. Lots of things have changed over the years, but there are still only 24 hours in a day. Time and energy are finite. The number of solutions is infinite. With a firm commitment, willingness to risk, and proper planning, you'll move right past those invisible barriers and into a promising future.

To me, it's well worth the risk that always accompanies working with another human being. In fact, I look at delegation as my only ticket to freedom. If I were micro-managing everything, I'd be glued to my computer and telephone every minute of the day. It's only because of my willingness to delegate that I'm able to live the laptop lifestyle. I work all over the world and have a blast doing it. If I didn't trust others enough to delegate, I'd just be working my life away—and I can't live that kind of life. You shouldn't settle for it either.

> ### POWER MOVE
> *Own your fears and excuses,*
> *and allow yourself to risk.*

For a traffic-generating, business building, outsourcing tip, go to http://123Employee. com/outsourcesmart/interview/02 or scan this QR code and watch this video now.

OUTSOURCING 101

3

Before we move on, let's talk about outsourcing basics. I thought about calling this chapter *Outsourcing for Dummies,* but if you're reading this book, you're no dummy. You're smart enough to find the information you need to free yourself from drudgery and live the lifestyle you want. In the last chapter, we went into detail about outsourcing. You may already be familiar with outsourcing. If so, you can skip this background information and move ahead to Chapter 4, where we talk about how to put this tool to work for your business. But for those who need it, here's a primer.

WHAT IS OUTSOURCING?

Most of us understand the "what" of outsourcing: outsourcing is a contractual relationship for the provision of business services by an external provider. In other words, a company pays another company to do some work.

Why Do Companies Outsource?

Outsourcing can reduce costs, increase service quality, and provide access to experts in specialized areas. Here are four more reasons that small businesses outsource.

Reason One: Because They Can

New information technologies make it easier than ever to hire, manage, and coordinate lower-cost, well-educated labor in the global economy, so cost-management as well as quality and time savings make outsourcing a good choice.

Reason Two: Because They Have To

As a business professional, you have to compete. If your competitors are going offshore to find technology or process support at drastically lower costs—and they are—doing the same becomes a no-brainer.

Reason Three: The Economy

Work is also being outsourced because of the recent global economic downturn. Companies are more focused than ever on improving their return on investments and managing spending. To find quality services at lower cost, companies are turning to outsourcing.

Reason Four: Freedom

Living the laptop lifestyle is all about freedom and flexibility, and so is outsourcing. Put more technically: outsourcing shifts fixed costs into variable costs. For example, it's much easier to scale back outsourced staff than internal staff.

Who's Doing It?

The financial industry led the way. In the 1990s, financial services firms (retail banking, investment banks, and insurance) began outsourcing. Firms like GE Capital, American Express, and Citigroup led the pack and were followed by Prudential, Merrill Lynch, J.P. Morgan Chase, Lehman Brothers, MetLife, Sallie Mae, Guardian Life, Conseco, and Bank of America.

Today, almost all major corporations outsource a portion of their marketing functions. But outsourcing is not just for the financial industry or the Fortune 500. Once thought of as an option only for large multinational corporations, outsourcing is now seen as a business solution for any organization interested in improving its market position and reducing costs. More and more, outsourcing is becoming a global business trend and one of the most powerful tools in the modernization of marketing.

The "Where" of Outsourcing

As of 2012, the five countries leading the outsourcing pack are India, the Philippines, Canada, Ireland, and Russia. Also on the "most popular" list are China, Mexico, and South Africa, followed by "the challengers": Brazil, the Caribbean region, Eastern Europe, Malaysia, Israel, Singapore, and Vietnam. Just below these are second-tier challengers: Northern Ireland, Bangladesh, Ghana, Korea, Mauritius, Nepal, Senegal, Sri Lanka, Taiwan, and Thailand.

So how do you choose the location that best fits your needs? Each outsourcing region has its own niche specialization:

- **China.** Research and development services for life sciences companies.

- **Sri Lanka.** Accounting services.

- **Singapore and Malaysia.** Financial and accounting and back-office processes.

- **Vietnam and Indonesia.** IT service providers.

- **India.** IT service. In the early 1990s, American Express, British Airways, and GE Capital used India for customer support and transaction processing. Why? India's education system generates 200,000 engineering and computer science graduates per year. Also, the Indian government gave a 10-year tax holiday for IT service companies in 2000 (which reduced the usual 36 percent tax to 15 percent).

- **The Philippines.** Contract support services. Recently, eTelecare and Ambergris Solutions have taken their BPO services here, and in 2012, the Tholons investment firm reported that the Philippines had surpassed India as the call center capital of the world, with an estimated 400,000 call center agents compared to India's 350,000. Tholons also included five cities in the Philippines in its list of the top 100 outsourcing destinations: Manila, Cebu, Davao, Santa Rosa, and Iloilo.

THE PHILIPPINES SUCCESS STORY

In 2009, Businessweek.com called the Philippines "more nimble than China or India" in outsourcing growth, and Mitchel Chang, site manager of Trend Micro, which in 2009 employed one-third of its total workforce in the Philippines, has said, "Filipino software professionals have an excellent service-oriented attitude, are responsive, passionate, and have strong English skills."

How the Philippines Learned from India

In the past decade, Filipinos made a conscious effort to emulate India's outsourcing success. At the height of India's success, Filipino officials visited India and studied its best practices. Based on India's model, the Filipino government fast-tracked the approval process for companies setting up call centers, offered tax breaks, accelerated the building permit process, and offered tax exemptions for computer and telecom equipment. Most importantly, government sponsored training helped 40,000 students improve their English and communication skills.

An Americanized Lifestyle

The Filipino's affinity for U.S. culture stems from the fact that the United States ruled the country from 1898 to 1946. In recent years, outsourcing service centers have changed both the rhythm and style of Filipino life. Young, nocturnal data center workers banter in English as easily as their native Tagalog and listen to American Top 40 and hip hop. After work they visit Americanized malls, bars, movie theaters, and cafés that have sprouted up near the centers. Thea Lu, a 30-year-old call-center team leader, says: "There used to be some doubt about letting young people work so late at night, but now this has become an industry that young people aspire to."

Infrastructure

India's biggest outsourcing hubs use diesel generators for electricity and struggle with attrition of up to 50 percent a year. Those problems inspired many American companies to look at the Philippines. In 2000, the California company "24/7 Customer" started outsourced operations in India but in 2005 opened an office in the Philippines. The company now has 4,000 employees in the Philippines and 3,000 in India. Its cofounder says, "It's very sad that India could not keep up with its neighbors."

Infrastructure projects are a major factor in the Philippines' growing popularity. Recently, a coal-fired power plant in the La Paz district stabilized its power supply and building developments in Cebu and Iloilo. The Filipino government has widened roads and linked cities to the airport. Residential and recreational areas are also being improved daily.

All of this progress has led to more efficient data centers with more floor space and technical advancements, such as cloud computing. The cloud allows facility managers to consolidate server space and consume less energy than traditional data centers.

In the Philippines, the outsourcing industry makes up about 6 percent of the gross domestic product. The Business Processing Association of the Philippines recorded $9 billion in revenues in 2010 and expects $25 billion in revenues by 2016.

WHAT'S BEING OUTSOURCED?

Outsourced work falls into three main categories: ITO, BPO, and KPO. Don't let the acronyms scare you. This is just the stuff you do every day.

- Information technology outsourcing (ITO) is technology-specific work, like managing network infrastructures and developing software applications. ITO has been around since Ross Perot founded EDS in 1962.

- Business process outsourcing (BPO) is all about service and refers to operational and administrative functions such as outbound calls, sales, client database, and payroll. It's typically used to execute duties: loan servicing, accounting, human resources, logistics, and procurement.

- Knowledge process outsourcing (KPO) is a subset of BPO. As its name suggests, KPO involves creativity of the mind. It typically involves research and analytics, but more recently it's come to include social networking, content production, legal work, research and development, design, online marketing, and search engine optimization.

KPO providers usually work more independently than BPO workers, who usually require more client direction. BPO and KPO used together make a great team. With today's constantly evolving technology, one outsourcing strategy doesn't come without the other.

Client Outsourcing Concerns

In 2011, 352 global bio-manufacturers ranked their top three outsourcing priorities. They represent universal concerns.

1. Stick to a schedule.

2. Establish a good working relationship.

3. Comply with my company's quality standards.

Why Should You Outsource?

Bill Gates has called outsourcing offshore "a common-sense proposition." But you don't have to take his word. Think about your company's needs. Outsourced marketing can help you if:

- You want a well-optimized and well-marketed website but don't have the time to create content on a regular schedule.

- You know that writing isn't your strength, but you realize that well-written content will help you build links and ranking.

- You're a good writer, but you have multiple websites or products that need content support, and you can't possibly write content for them all.

In case you'd like a little nudge, here are a couple of testimonials from professionals who outsource their social media marketing:

- **Bardi Toto, Social Marketing Strategist.** "My assistant has built up my groups on Facebook and my fan pages. I now have over 2,500 people in my groups and as fans. I could not have done it without my VA."

- **Larry Goins, Real Estate Investment Trainer.** "I gotta tell you, you have to get a VA. They can do everything you need: manage your social media, your social network, your Facebook, your Twitter account, post videos, submit articles, answer your e-mails. Oh my God, I used to spend half a day answering my e-mail."

- **Robert Lord, Direct Source Millionaire.** "I've been outsourcing my social media for about nine months now, and believe it or not, my Facebook has exploded and my Twitter has exploded. I can't believe the amount of work and time and effort these guys put into my accounts. I feel like they are my very own employees, and I absolutely love them."

They sound happy to me. What do you think?

Outsourcing Your Admin

I'm going to be bold and say that *any* business—large, small, or sole proprietor—would benefit from outsourcing administrative tasks. They're tedious, time consuming, and sometimes, they can be over your head. With new applications surfacing daily, it would be impossible for you to learn to apply them with any degree of competence and still run your business efficiently.

Outsourcing doesn't have to cut deeply into your budget if you outsource smart. You'd benefit even by outsourcing two to three hours a week to a competent VA. Trust me, that'll be enough to hook you. Once you see that bottom line begin to creep up, you'll be even more motivated to invest in your business, and you'll look for more tasks to delegate.

Think about how many hours you spend returning phone calls, responding to e-mails, organizing data, filing digital material, maintaining your database (remember, the gold mine), and maintaining customer relations. Those are all basic tasks common among most businesspeople. They can all be done by someone else.

What that means is, for every hour you delegate, you have one more hour in your week for marketing, sales, promotion, and other IGAs. Ask yourself how you think your business would be impacted by three extra hours a week for the tasks that actually make you money? There's your answer.

If you make $50 an hour in your business, delegating three hours gives you the potential to earn an additional $150 a week, $600 a month, $7,800 a year. Have any ideas what you might do with that chunk of change? That's the amount of revenue you're turning away by hoarding your tasks. Ouch!

Administrative VAs are a good investment because they charge by the minute. Some use specialized software to calculate the exact number of minutes they work on your project, and that's what you pay for. Sometimes you'll pay a per-project rate based on an estimate of the time it'll take to execute tasks. Either way, you're still ahead of the game.

As with other professionals, if VAs want to stay in business, they need to provide impeccable service. They'll want to retain you as a client, so you can be assured of excellence. Their industry requires a strong knowledge of Internet applications and new technologies, so good VAs stay up to date. Who also benefits? You do. You don't have to learn new apps if you don't want to, and, in some cases, you don't even have to buy certain programs to get the benefit of their use. Your VA will often have what you need.

Okay, so that's the *why* in our discussion of outsourcing administrative tasks. Here's a little more detail about the *what*. Aside from the tasks mentioned in the first part of our discussion and in other areas of *Outsource Smart*, there are advantages to delegating these other tasks:

- Creating forms and spreadsheets

- Research (competitors, new products, new ideas)

- PowerPoint presentations

- Bill payments

- Looking for images, links, content ideas, etc.

- Dealing with personal things like birthdays, gifts, and special remembrances

- Travel arrangements

Be as detailed as possible with your VA. Clearly communicate your goals and expectations as well as any deadlines. All that's left to decide is the *when*.

For a traffic-generating, business building, outsourcing tip, go to http://123Employee. com/outsourcesmart/interview/03 or scan this QR code and watch this video now.

HOW TO HIRE AND TRAIN AN OUTSOURCED VA

4

FREELANCE OR FACILITY?

The first decision when you're considering using an out-sourced VA is whether to hire a freelancer on your own or to go through a managed facility; an organization that helps business owners procure and manage virtual assistants located overseas.

Your decision depends on what kinds of tasks you're looking to delegate as well as the time you plan to spend on interviewing and training. If you're looking for someone to work on a part-time basis, a freelancer is probably your best option. Although some managed facilities allow clients to hire part-time workers, most do not.

PROJECT WORK

Project work is something that can easily be delegated to a free-lance VA. For example, a freelancer would be appropriate for organizing a mail campaign, creating a spreadsheet, or preparing

a PowerPoint presentation. The project should be short in dura-
tion, however, and one that can be explained with a set of simple
directions.

The temporary nature of project work takes some of the
risk out of hiring a freelancer. The rationale is simple: when you
don't have time to do extensive interviewing or training, a brief,
termination-at-will arrangement makes the most sense. Hiring a
freelancer can also be a great way to "try out" the concept of using
an outsourced VA without committing to a managed facility. If one
VA doesn't work out, you're easily free of the relationship.

FINDING A VA

One of the best ways to find people to do business with is the
age-old method of seeking referrals. Depending on the task or
project, contact business associates who may be able to help you
out, including past clients. For example, if you're part of a Web
design firm and need content, search your records for any writers
you've worked with in the past. Is there anyone you've provided
products or services for who's skilled in the area in which you
now require support? By simply searching your database, you
may find the perfect provider right under your nose.

If not, ask professionals you trust if there's anyone they'd
recommend. Word gets around. Maybe there's also a provider
they'd advise you to shy away from. Networking groups are a
great resource for referrals. Just make sure you're being referred
to someone because she provides quality work and not just
because she's a member of the group.

If the task you want to outsource is industry specific, you may
want to ask others in your industry if they know of providers you
can call on. This is one of the reasons it's advantageous to build
relationships with people in your niche. There's a good chance
you're not the only one in your industry who outsources projects.

By asking clients as well as business associates, you may find either they've outsourced a similar project in the past, or you may hear the same referral name more than once. Finding a provider either way allows for feedback from your source. You may be able to see examples of their work and get a good idea of the quality you can expect to receive.

Placing a classified ad in a newspaper, on a job board, or on your website is another way to find a provider. Advertising puts your name in front of a large number of people without having to put in too much work. You can request resumés or information via e-mail. Weed out all of the subpar applicants and list the providers you think can give you what you want.

Online Sources for Freelancers

Some Internet companies specialize in connecting businesses with service providers. The majority of companies planning to outsource aspects of their businesses go this route. The main advantage to using these sites is that you never have to pay a dime to list your project. Simply list your project and wait for providers to come to you. After your project has been posted, providers will bid on your services. Bids include price points, turnaround time, and a short proposal that outlines experience. Most online sites will allow providers to send samples of their work to prove their competence.

If you're going to use one of these sites, remember to carefully post your project. Providers are going to bid based on what your ad says. If you leave out key details, they're not going to be able to give you an accurate proposal.

There are a lot of these sites, but the industry leaders are elance.com, guru.com, and getafreelancer.com. All three sites have thousands of members who'll bid on your project. When you're just starting out, they'll provide a low-cost, low-risk vehicle on the outsourcing path.

Where to Find a Freelancer Online

You can find freelancers through the following websites:

- **Craigslist.** Craigslist allows you to post a free ad in almost any city in the world. To find a freelancer in the United States, go to craigslist.com and choose your city. To choose an outsourced freelancer from craigslist.com, choose "cl worldwide" and then select from among the following regions: Africa, Americas, Asia, Europe, Middle East, or Oceania.

   To find a worker in the Philippines, choose "Asia" and then "Philippines." From there, select a city. On the page of the city (e.g., Manila), click on "Translate" to convert the page into English. It allows you to place an ad exactly as you would if you were seeking a worker in the United States.

- **Bestjobs.ph.** This site allows free job advertising to thousands of Filipino employees. You can also do a resumé search using keywords or create a web page in the employer directory section to promote your business.

- **Odesk.com.** Odesk.com is currently the largest site for remote work, offering access to more than one million qualified contractors. Here, workers bid for projects, and payment is made through the site. Work is guaranteed. A feature called "Work Diary" allows you to monitor your employee's work in progress at any time.

- **Elance.com.** Elance.com is a slightly upscale version of Odesk.com. Programming, marketing, creative, and administrative contractors are available to bid on your projects. These workers are available for a variety of projects, including code writing, crafting a marketing plan, designing your website, and managing your day-to-day schedule. As with Odesk.com, you post a job, receive competing bids, then hire, monitor, and pay for the work (which is guaranteed) online.

- **Guru.com.** Guru.com, founded as emoonlighter.com in 1998, has grown significantly in popularity as a freelance marketplace, both with freelance service providers and those seeking services. Along with getafreelancer.com, guru.com is putting many a student through college as quickly as they're lowering the price point for freelance services across the board.

- **vWorker.com.** Through this agency, you post your project, receive bids from workers, choose your worker, and deposit payment in escrow. After the work is done, you receive and approve the work and then pay and rate your worker. vWorker.com offers a money-back guarantee if the worker "fudges the time card, bills you for time not worked," or doesn't deliver work "to contract, on time, or on budget."

    vWorker.com also allows you to choose your "economy" and English proficiency preferences. If you choose a worker from an "emerging economy" (e.g., Romania, India, China, etc.), the price is often 40 to 80 percent cheaper than if you opt for a worker from a mature economy (e.g., United States, Western Europe, or Australia).

WHEN TO CHOOSE AN OUTSOURCING MANAGED FACILITY

After experimenting with freelance VAs, you may get to a point where you're ready to take the leap and hire a dedicated assistant. That's the time to go with a managed facility. You might also decide to use a managed facility based on a number of other factors.

Time Zone Issues

I've seen many entrepreneurs who started with freelancers and then moved to managed facilities after becoming frustrated with the distance; they found they couldn't adequately monitor an overseas employee. When deciding between a freelancer or managed facility, keep the time zone issue in mind. The worker's time zone may not match yours very closely. In fact, it may be nighttime for the worker when it is morning for you, and this mismatch can hinder communication. Time zone issues are not a problem with managed facilities, as they're set up to enable communication with you, the client, during normal working hours.

Virtual Communication

Use Skype to Communicate

Communication needs to flow easily and efficiently if you're going to see the value in working with VAs, domestic or international. Time differences can sometimes be a challenge, but if you're working with a quality company, the VA will be available to you at your convenience, in your time zone.

Depending on your personality, skill level, and project requirements, there are several methods of communication to choose from. My advice would be to make sure your technological communication skill level matches or surpasses that of competitors, or you may find yourself eating their dust. Technology waits for no one to catch up. It will continue to evolve whether or not you get it. Get it?

One common method of communication used by both domestic and international companies is Skype. Skype is a service that allows users to communicate over the Internet by voice, video, and instant messaging. Registering for Skype is simple. Just go to the website and follow the prompts to register. You'll be asked to pick a unique Skype name, which your contacts will use to locate you. Using instant messaging or voice chat (with or without video), you and your contacts will connect with each other at no charge anywhere on the planet, through your computers. With a paid subscription, you can also use Skype like a telephone and call mobile phones and land lines across all boundaries. The sound quality is so clear, it'll feel like the person you're talking with is in the next room. Some radio shows use Skype for remote guests, and listeners can't tell if the person is in the studio or on the phone.

The cost of subscriptions is so low it's almost insane. At the time of this writing, unlimited domestic calling costs $2.99 a month and international calling is $12.99. Like I said, insane.

Skype voice chat also allows conference calling, and text chat allows group chats. You can store chat history and edit previous messages. If you're a regular instant message user, you'll find additional features that are familiar to you.

You can also purchase Skype credit if you don't want an unlimited usage subscription. SkypeIn, an online number service, allows you to receive calls on your computer placed by conventional phone subscribers to a local Skype phone number. Local numbers are available for a host of countries, including, of course, the United Kingdom and the United States. You can have local numbers in other countries. Calls to the numbers are charged at the same rates as calls to fixed lines in the specified countries. Skype is still cheaper than conventional phone service.

With the proper Skype setup, you can video conference with your team no matter where in the world your team members are. Now this will rock your world, outsourcers. No more taking short vacations because of meetings you can't miss. If you have a broadband connection, you can video conference from anywhere on the globe, bringing your network of workers, partners, and clients together. Just remember, if you don't want your clients or associates to know you're on vacation, you may not want to use the beach as a backdrop.

However, if you lead a team of direct sales professionals, just imagine how motivating it would be for you to conference in from some exotic location and for them to see you relaxing and enjoying benefits of the success you've worked toward in your business. It would surely inspire me. Oh, remember the Mai Tai. Sipping on a tropical drink really cements the concept.

Don't have video capability on your computer? If you don't have a webcam, you can audio conference. At the time of this writing, Skype audio conferences currently support up to 25 people at a time, including the host.

If you're thinking of trashing the landline in favor of Skype, keep in mind that it doesn't provide the ability to call 911 in the United States, 999 in Canada, or other emergency numbers. Have an analog line available as a backup. If the electricity goes out or Internet issues arise, your cell phone is worthless.

Another reason to go with a managed facility is that trained workers disappear. Managed facilities have a higher retention rate, along with increased accountability. A potential problem is the lack of infrastructure in developing countries. In many, blackouts and brownouts are common. For example, it's common for the power to go out every day in the Philippines. When a VA is working from home and the power goes out, there can be a disastrous loss of productivity. Conversely, if the Internet goes out in a managed facility, there's backup power as well as redundant systems for consistent Internet. Which brings us to phone support.

Phone Support

I don't recommend using freelancers for phone support. It generally doesn't work, and I don't see it working for quite some time. Why? Simply put: infrastructure issues. Even in areas in which workers have broadband at home, it's usually not reliable enough to support consistent, solid, clear-sounding phone service. For phone support, make sure you use a managed facility where the bandwidth is high, the connection is redundant, and power is not an issue.

When you use a managed facility, at the end of each day you should receive a call distribution report detailing each call. Some facilities will also provide recordings so you can hear each call and use them for coaching or training. These facilities will generally be using VOIP (voice over Internet protocol). Another benefit of managed facilities for phone support is automatic dialing. In a facility that uses a dialer, a list of phone numbers is uploaded so that the call is connected automatically. When someone picks up, the VA sees a name on the screen and begins to converse. When you take the dialing out of the agent's hands, you increase production tremendously. This is difficult if not impossible to do when using a freelancer.

Putting Systems in Place

You might decide to go with a managed facility because you're ready for a single worker who understands and is committed to your business. Emotional investment comes only over time, and a dedicated VA who can grow with your business is more readily available through a managed facility. Because there is always management on site to supervise your VA, you don't have to be there.

Possibly the biggest advantage to using a managed facility is that training is taken out of the equation. You decide which category of pre-trained VA would best suit your purposes— someone trained in computer programming, phones, answering e-mail, blogging, accounting, etc.—and then leave the training to the system. Remember: outsourcing smart is all about putting systems in place, and a managed facility is one kind of system that can allow you to be less hands-on so you can focus on the big picture.

AGREEMENTS AND NEGOTIATIONS

When you do anything, the goal is to have as positive an experience as possible, and that includes outsourcing. Handling a few things at the beginning of your relationship with a VA will minimize the likelihood of any major problems down the road. One reason companies and providers experience friction is they don't deal with potential issues up front. Because they feel uncomfortable, some people leave too much unsaid when they begin a new relationship. Developing good communication skills will help you avoid falling into this trap.

The Money Conversation

One of the hardest things to talk about is also one of the most important pieces of business to handle at the outset: money. In any business transaction, money changes hands. Before you begin outsourcing—whether to an independent contractor or to a service provider—the first thing both of you will need to do is agree upon a fair price. In some cases, this won't be negotiable on one or both sides. Some VAs have a price and they stick to it. If you want to haggle, the next word you'll hear out of their mouths will be, "Next!" They're not willing to budge. The ball is then in your court. Is working with this person worth his asking price, or can you move on and look for a comparable professional at a lower price-point?

Although hourly rates are often firm, many VAs and independent contractors are willing to negotiate when a flat fee or quote is requested. On most occasions, it'll take a couple of offers and counteroffers to find a price both you and the contractor feel is fair.

After both of you have agreed to a price for the project, provide a written agreement and make sure it gets signed! This is so important. Thousands of outsourced projects get completed without a written agreement in place. Not good. Even though we'd like to take people at their word, and even though it's possible to do business without an agreement or contract, both sides put themselves at risk.

In your agreement, financial terms should be clearly stated. Include the total payment of the project as well as any overtime payments you've agreed upon. Also, make sure the agreement states when payment will be made, the timing and amount of any deposits (refundable or nonrefundable), and the preferred method of payment. There are lots of payment options available such as check, money order, bank transfer, or online systems such as PayPal.

Will you be responsible for paying expenses for overtime or revisions, or are you paying a flat rate, inclusive of ancillary costs? You and your VA or contractor can agree upon this in a couple of ways. You can decide that the overall payment for the project includes all revisions and any overtime hours, if hours are even a factor. If your provider isn't comfortable with this, you can discuss another payment structure, such as an hourly rate or a per-revision rate. Each structure has its advantages and disadvantages for either party. One thing that's not negotiable is that payment arrangements must be outlined up front.

Timelines

When you outsource a project, unless it's an ongoing service, you'll likely have a time frame and completion date in mind. Discuss this in advance with your VA in order to avoid mistakes and setbacks. Not only will a timeline be beneficial to you, but your service provider will need direction in setting aside the appropriate amount of time to complete the project. These details, along with scheduled reviews, should also be in writing.

OUTSOURCING WRITING

When you're outsourcing copywriting and ghostwriting, time-lines can be extremely important. You'll also need to establish how files will be exchanged (usually via e-mail attachments) and to make clear your desired format. The most popular are Microsoft Word documents, plain text documents, and PDF files.

The same holds true when dealing with software projects. Make clear to your provider up front how you expect to transfer the work or you may discover too late incompatibilities between your provider's software and yours. That can be a really expensive oversight.

How to Set Your Price

Whenever you're talking money, the main consideration is that both sides need a fair deal. A deal in which one side gets a far better value is slated for trouble from the beginning. If the provider thinks she is not getting paid enough, she usually won't put forth her best effort. And if you feel you're paying too much, you might be resentful and vow never to work with that person again. Finding a happy medium is the best way to ensure a successful project.

So if you're new at outsourcing, how do you determine what you're willing to pay for services? Yeah, I know, it can be hard to make that first payment to someone else when you've been doing the task for "free" for years. I want to tell you, you have not. Every hour you spend on tasks that don't move your business forward costs you dearly—probably more than you'll ever spend on outsourcing. If you calculate the number of hours you spend doing detail work when you could be growing your business, you'll see my point.

An experienced VA will have his own guidelines and rates. You, on the other hand, have your budget to consider. The first thing you'll do is communicate the project details to the VA. In most cases, the VA will issue a proposal outlining the total cost of the project. If you're looking for ongoing support in a particular area, the proposal will be different than one for a per-project quote.

You or the VA may need to modify the proposal to find common ground. If the VA's price is higher than your budget will allow and you still want to work with this person, you may want to make a counteroffer. Don't be surprised if the VA makes another counteroffer. Once you both agree to the terms, you're good to go. As long as both parties bear in mind the position of the other, you can build a good relationship. You, as a professional, have a budget to stick to, and your VA, also a professional, needs to make a living. A win-win situation supports both of you.

If you're going to be highly successful outsourcing your tasks, you've got to learn how to be a good negotiator. Even if you're a small business owner or, for that matter, a one-person business, knowing what you're worth, what you want, and how to get it will prepare you to be successful in the business world. When you're negotiating, keep these tips in mind:

1. Be fair with others, and the world will be fair with you. As they say, "What goes around comes around." You'll also have more self-respect if you're fair with others.

2. Keep an open mind. People who see things only their own way cheat themselves out of another point of view. When negotiating, take into account the other person's reasoning. You may have overlooked something.

3. Make reasonable requests, especially when it comes to timelines. You may have needed something yesterday, and that's why you're outsourcing, but if you couldn't get it done by the deadline, keep in mind that a VA (who works

with other clients) would also be challenged to finish the job quickly. Be realistic, and be willing to reward rush jobs.

4. Be willing to compromise. You and your VA may be on opposite ends of the field where compensation is concerned, but you aim for a common goal. Exercise a little give-and-take when it comes to financial arrangements. Take each other's circumstances and proposals into account, and meet in the middle.

5. Always be professional during the negotiation process. From time to time, buttons get pushed. Even if the VA becomes rude or sarcastic—*or worse*—remain professional. You can't take anything back once you've said it. You can apologize, but sometimes that's not enough. When you remain calm and respectful, oftentimes your demeanor can turn another person around. That doesn't mean you need to take abuse.

6. There's no shame in walking away from the deal. You don't need to agree to a situation that doesn't work for you. If, however, you agree to an arrangement and decide to walk away, make sure the person is adequately compensated for the time they've lost.

Written agreements and clear communication are essential for good working relationships. Follow the guidelines above, and your experiences with outsourcing will not only be professionally worthwhile but personally gratifying as well.

THE HIRING PROCESS

If you're hiring an outsourced freelancer on your own, it's very possible that you won't speak to candidates during the hiring process. In fact, you might never speak to the worker you ultimately hire to complete your project. If you go through a service like vWorker.com, some vetting of candidates is done for you. If you use a job board like Craigslist, you'll have to assess the skills and veracity of potential employees yourself. Technology can help. Skype is the second best thing to an in-person interview, and phone interviewing is the third best.

It's possible that neither of these will be viable options. The reality of hiring outsourced freelancers is that they often work from home and have limited bandwidth, slow Internet, or an inability to access Skype. If this becomes an obstacle, you may want to choose a managed facility, which will have systems in place to overcome infrastructure limitations. You may be able to interact with candidates via Skype chat, and you'll certainly be able to e-mail them. Some facilities allow you to interview candidates by phone.

Interview Questions

Whether you use a freelancer or a managed facility, you'll want to ask specific questions of your candidates, geared toward your business. Imagine yourself hiring someone local; what questions would you ask? In an outsourcing scenario, you'll have a little more leeway.

In the United States, you're legally barred from asking candidates about their age, family, and children. In the Philippines, such questions are permissible, and you may want to take advantage of the opportunity to ask them. For example, you might see hiring someone with a family as desirable. To you, a family may indicate stability and the ability to commit. It might also be seen as an earning incentive. On the other hand, if you're looking for someone who can work odd hours or be on call, a worker with family obligations might not be ideal. The point is, in many countries, you're permitted to take those kinds of factors into consideration. You might also consider the gender of a candidate.

Perhaps you want a female voice to greet customers; having that criterion is not taboo.

The Task-Oriented Interview

Making a hiring decision is a huge responsibility, and you may enter into it with understandable fears. "What if I hire someone who lacks the necessary skills to complete the project?" Many employers hire blind, taking the candidate's word for the information they provide. The interview session goes something like this:

"Are you proficient with Windows?"

"Yes, I am."

"How fast do you type?"

"I type well over 60 words per minute."

The interviewer then decides whether to believe or disbelieve those responses based on a resumé, a few chats with references he doesn't know, and his intuition. And then he takes a leap of faith.

I believe leaps of faith are necessary in any business—but not when it comes to the hiring process. You can ask candidates if they're proficient with a particular software program or able to write a paragraph in fluent English, and take their word for it— or you can test these proficiencies before you hire. The best way to ensure you hire someone who can complete a task capably is to—you guessed it—give them a task and see whether they can complete it capably.

I recommend making a small task (or two or three) part of the interview process. When I interview someone who will be writing for me, I have them write for me. I might ask them to write a paragraph about why I should hire them, or to write a paragraph that summarizes our phone interview.

Heed Red Flags

If you want someone who's going to be dedicated to your business, you'll need to heed any warning signs. Red flags include candidates who won't allow you to communicate with them directly, candidates who don't have any work history, and candidates who are hesitant about giving you references.

If you're using a service such as vWorker.com, you'll want to make sure the candidates have decent test scores and ratings and that the testimonials they provide are real (not self-generated). Look for someone who has a good track record and a history of satisfied customers. If you use a managed facility, candidates are prescreened, and the company will provide you with references. But it's still your responsibility to contact those references and choose the best candidate for the job.

Trust Your Gut

Intuition has its place in the hiring process, but even intuition has its learning curve. The more hiring you do, the easier it is to trust your gut. Don't go only by the numbers. Skills-testing is fine, but remember that skills can be improved, whereas character is ingrained. Don't choose a candidate who types 70 words per minute but has an unfriendly or defensive demeanor over someone you click with instantly who types only 60 words per minute.

I've hired hundreds of people over the years, and today I have several hundred employees. I typically hire someone after a one- or two-minute interview. If I know the candidate's qualifications and I know what's needed in a particular position, I can tell after talking to her for just a few minutes whether she'll work out.

This is what I've learned: I can put a candidate through intricate testing, but if my gut says it's not a good fit, that's what takes precedence. I've had people achieve top scores when testing, only to leave a month after being hired, and I've seen people with heart struggle at the beginning, getting better and better through sheer perseverance until they end up among my top, most trusted managers. If you're an entrepreneur, you're probably used to trusting your instincts, so put them to use in making hiring decisions—but don't do so blindly. Use task-interviewing and common sense, and respect the red flags.

TRAINING FOR THE DELEGATION-PHOBIC

Now that you've decided which tasks need delegation, decided whether to go with a freelancer or managed facility, and hired your VA, it's time for everyone's least favorite task: training. You'd be surprised how often overworked entrepreneurs tell me they've ruled out using a VA because of the "impossibility" of training someone at a distance. With today's technology, that excuse doesn't fly.

For those entrepreneurs who dread training, I'm sorry, but I have to use the same "tough love" approach you use with your teenager and say again: get over it. Remember how badly you want your freedom? Remember how you want to live the laptop lifestyle? Well, keeping that in mind will help you work through your resistance and read on with an open mind. If you want to free yourself, training others is key. Let's break down the many possible methods of training an overseas VA, from best to worst.

Best Training Method: Video

My favorite way to train is by using screen recording and video editing software to make screen-capture videos. I like video because I believe in the "train once" principle. Conducting the same training session twice is the definition of wasted time, and with the technology available today, it's unnecessary. With video training, you don't have to conduct the same live training over and over. The VA can watch it repeatedly.

Training videos act as attrition insurance. In the people business, sometimes you lose your people. If you have a training system in place, it's not a disaster because you don't have to do another live training.

Using video also allows you to achieve consistency in training. It's fast, efficient, and perfect for VAs with whom you have no daily voice communication. Why is it efficient? Because you can use one video to train multiple employees. You create a training video once and you don't have to train over and over again. And if you lose an employee, you can just give the new employee the same training video. In effect, you turn yourself into McDonald's. If you go into McDonald's in Beijing, a burger and fries taste exactly the same as they do in Los Angeles. That's because there's a system in place. If you have a training system—if you record videos for every aspect of training in your business—you can ensure that the quality is consistent.

What if you hire a couple of VAs, they start doing daily tasks, and you find they're making mistakes? You can simply say: "Go back to the video." In fact, the VA can do this on an ongoing basis. If you give your VAs unlimited access to training videos, you'll find that they're eager to become competent and will review the training videos as much as is necessary. Everyone remembers being new at a job; it's an uncomfortable feeling. You have questions, but you're embarrassed to ask them because you think they might have been answered during training, and you don't want to seem incompetent. A training video that can be watched repeatedly is the answer. Typically, conscientious VAs will view training videos until they become experts at their assigned tasks.

Recording the Training Video

How do you record videos? For a Mac user, it's easy to do so using QuickTime or Screenflow. The online tutorials walk you through the process, and render time is short. Using QuickTime, simply open the program, hit "file" at the top of your screen, and select the option that allows you to "record your screen." The render time is negligible. You can shoot an hour-long video and render a training video in a few minutes.

If you're using a PC, Camtasia Studio works well and comes with a 30-day trial. The downside is that a long training video can take hours to render. A one-hour video can take four or five hours to render, making your computer unavailable for anything else during that chunk of time.

This isn't a problem if you do short training sessions, between one and 20 minutes. You'll want to break training into short sessions anyway to keep your new employee's attention.

Screen Capture Video

Creating a training video does not require that you sit down, comb your hair, and get ready for your close-up—although you could do it that way. For a training video, you're less concerned about the final product being stylish or entertaining and more concerned about content. Screen capture video captures both audio (your voice) and visuals (the moves you're making on your computer screen), allowing you to explain and demonstrate procedures simultaneously.

Audio Recording

Recording audio only is another option for entrepreneurs who are just too busy to sit down and think about visuals. I often record training videos during my downtime—while waiting for a connecting flight at an airport, or even while on an airplane. If you use this option, though, be ready to explain to the flight attendant that you're recording only and not involved in a two-way conversation. (And yes, you'll be questioned just as frequently when sitting in first class, with the other laptop lifestylers.) To use the audio-only method, speak into your iPhone, save the files, then sync them to your computer and send them out to your VAs.

Software Tutorials

Why reinvent the wheel? If you need your VAs to become proficient on a specific software program, have them sit down with that program's tutorial. If they need to master the use of an online shopping cart such as 1ShoppingCart.com and Infusionsoft, or an e-mail system like Constant Contact or AWeber, they all come with tutorial videos. Just give your VA access to the tutorial video and you're done.

The Training Manual

The most conventional training method is the training manual. Creating these tools can be time consuming, but they can be duplicated and shared easily. However, make sure you keep an electronic version for updates. There's nothing more frustrating and time-wasting than having to retype a massive training manual because it needs to be updated and someone has lost the Word file or flash drive.

Personally, I find training manuals to be insufferable. Odds are, so will your new employees, and you don't want them hating their new jobs from the get-go. If you have to go the "sit down and read this" training route, you might want to at least turn your manual into a PowerPoint slideshow by breaking the text into small chunks and adding some visuals. Trainees won't absorb or retain what they can't sit through.

In-Person Training

If you want to be "old school" about it, in-person training is also an option. It's lowest on my list of preferred methods, though, because I find it to be risky. You might provide the best training session in the world for your key manager, but what happens when your key manager leaves without training a replacement? Like I said: risky.

Backwards Planning

As with any effective business strategy, the key is backwards planning. Begin with your desired outcome in mind and work backwards. If the outcome is a well-trained employee, how do you make that happen? My first preference is always video, then audio, then a written manual, then, as a last resort, an in-person session.

Training for Specific Tasks: Accounting

KPO (knowledge process outsourcing) is big overseas, particularly in India. You can typically hire bookkeepers for $10 to $15 per hour and CPAs for less than $40 per hour who are just as competent as American workers. In fact, many CPA firms and tax preparation firms outsource to Indian companies.

Managed facilities have trained bookkeepers, but if you want to go with a freelancer, don't let training be an obstacle. It's not difficult to train an employee with basic accounting knowledge to do standard bookkeeping. You can have your VA go to Quick-Books, watch the tutorials, and then show her how you use the application in your business.

Training for Specific Tasks: Computer Tech

My friend Tim is a computer technician who repairs hardware and software. He charges $150 an hour, and his time is money. The more billable hours he has, the more income he has. So if he were to do his own billing, even if it took him only an hour, he'd lose out on $150. A few years ago, Tim hired a VA named Lito. Now, after Tim wraps up with a client, he texts the info to Lito. Lito immediately creates an invoice in QuickBooks, e-mails the invoice to the client, and sends Tim a copy. Meanwhile, Tim moves on to the next customer. Lito handles collections as well, following up with clients and making notes on accounts.

Recently, Tim has trained Lito to do some tech support, fixing computers using a virtual desktop. Tim could hire a sales force of repair people to work with him in the United States, but he knows the risk. Those people, once trained, could eventually become his competition or even steal his clients and undercut him; those are the business realities. But with Lito doing virtual repairs, Tim never has to worry about Lito stealing his clients. Lito has no direct interaction with clients, and he's an ocean away. Oh, yeah, by the way—Lito knew nothing about accounting. He learned everything from the QuickBooks online tutorial.

Training for Specific Tasks: E-mail

Can you use a freelancer to answer your e-mail? Sure. For the first couple weeks, it's a good idea to get together with your VA on Skype and do a few screen share sessions. Recently, I helped a business owner friend, Wendy, train her VA, Aubrey, to answer her e-mails. They started out with a few weekly Skype sessions in which Wendy answered her e-mails while explaining to Aubrey what she was doing and why she was doing it. She showed Aubrey how to identify spam and how to save and consolidate so that all incoming e-mail would be sorted into the appropriate folders. Aubrey maintained a second, private account and showed Aubrey how to determine which e-mails were time-sensitive or important enough to transfer into that personal account.

Within a month, Aubrey had taken over, and Wendy was free. Now, Aubrey answers those e-mails she can, consolidates the rest by topic, and forwards those that are important and timely to Wendy. At the end of each day, Aubrey sends Wendy one e-mail. That one e-mail contains about 10 or 15 e-mails, but over time, as Aubrey becomes more proficient at identifying what needs to be forwarded, that e-mail will shrink. I currently receive zero forwarded e-mails from L.J., who is my executive assistant in the Philippines. Can you imagine receiving only one e-mail a day? How much could you get done every day if you didn't have to worry about e-mail? That's what I call freedom!

Have you attended seminars or events and been so inspired you bought a learning system but have done nothing with it? You know it has value, but you just can't get to it. How about letting your VA learn it? Your business will benefit without you spending the time, and your VA will immediately become more valuable. It's like eating a hot fudge sundae without the calories!

For a traffic-generating, business building, outsourcing tip go to http://123Employee. com/outsourcesmart/interview/04, or scan this QR code and watch this video now.

LEGAL AND FINANCIAL REALITIES—HOW TO MANAGE AN OUTSOURCED VIRTUAL ASSISTANT

5

Congratulations! You've overcome your fear of outsourcing, hired one or more overseas virtual assistants, and trained them with your choice of videos, manuals, and/or in-person sessions. The next step is monitoring your new employees during the crucial period as they're "learning the ropes." But how can you do that from a distance? Let me walk you through some effective ways.

MONITORING YOUR OUTSOURCED VA

Monitoring and managing are two different things. You'll need to do both throughout your relationship with an outsourced VA, but let's begin with monitoring, the system by which you make sure you've chosen a suitable employee—one with both the ability level and personal integrity you need.

Webcam Monitoring

Now you're scared. Aren't webcams set up in girls' locker rooms by Peeping Toms? Now that I've planted that image in your brain, erase it! Webcam monitoring may seem distasteful, and it's not a practice you would typically use with an onsite employee, but it's an accepted and even expected practice when dealing with VAs who are half a world away.

A workplace webcam is not sleazy, and it's not even covert. The new employee is typically aware that her workstation is being monitored by the off-site employer. Here's how it works: During and for some time after your VA's training period, you as the employer set up a webcam during your employee's work hours. A tiny box on your computer screen allows you to see that your employee or employees are at their desks doing their thing. Several types of programs are available for this purpose, including "Webwatcher." Once your employees prove themselves diligent, or if they're uncomfortable about being monitored in this way, you can pull back.

I used this method during the training of my first outsourced employee, Carl. I set up a remote desktop and checked in to see what he was doing during the breaks between training sessions. What he was doing was typing up his notes. That told me everything I needed to know about Carl, and he turned out to be an amazing employee.

Daily Reports

If you just can't shake the *perv* feeling enough to monitor your VAs via webcam, another way of monitoring progress is with end-of-day reports. During the initial training period or on an ongoing basis, you can have your VAs provide you with detailed reports at the end of each workday. Does this create another daily task for you? No, because you won't have to check the reports daily. You can check them weekly or periodically—just often enough to reassure yourself that your VAs are completing the tasks they've been assigned at the quality level you require.

At a managed outsourcing facility, VA monitoring is done for you. You'll have a project manager on site whose job it is to supervise your employees and guarantee their productivity. The best part about this method? It brings you one step closer to being free.

Documentation

Remember when I said that monitoring is not the same as managing? One way to think of the difference: monitoring is temporary or intermittent, and management is ongoing. And since management is ongoing, it involves that dreaded legal reality: documentation. You may already have a hiring contract, review, and termination system in place for your onsite employees. If so, you may not need to alter your system for VAs. But if you're an entrepreneur whose only employee is an outsourced VA, I've provided some sample documents at the end of this chapter that you can personalize for your own management needs. They include:

- Company policies
- Virtual assistant work for hire agreement
- Virtual assistant daily time report
- Virtual assistant no pass performance review—termination
- Virtual assistant pass performance review
- Virtual assistant performance warning

Protecting Your Business Secrets

If your project involves intellectual property (IP) you need to protect, the worker's country may not have any laws that are enforceable to protect it. As an extreme example: an unethical worker might try to resell your IP to others, and you might not be able to enforce a nondisclosure agreement or sue them for damages. If this is a concern, consult with your attorney concerning the IP laws in the countries you are considering, and choose one with laws in place that will protect your interests.

Reasonable Versus Unreasonable Suspicions

I'm often asked about the safety of sharing business secrets with outsourced VAs, a concern that reminds me of the Yellow Peril, also referred to as Yellow Terror. In 1855, at the height of the California Gold Rush, the largest immigrant group in the United States happened to be the Chinese. Seen as competition for gold and wages in the newly industrialized nation, Asians began to be depicted in Yellow Peril literature as cold, greedy, and secretive. This paranoia ultimately resulted in legislation that blocked Chinese immigration for a decade and established negative stereotypes that took years to break down. It's important to distinguish between legitimate fears and needless suspicion, which in some cases is the result of cultural stereotyping.

I believe that your business secrets are as safe, if not safer, in the hands of a foreign virtual assistant than with your in-house domestic employees. The fact that your foreign workers have fewer resources than you have means they also have fewer opportunities to use any proprietary information they may gain in the course of their employment with you.

Task Arbitrage

There's no need to agonize over whether your fears are legitimate or baseless if you practice good business security in the first place. It's safest to avoid sharing your deepest, darkest business secrets with *any* of your employees. Task arbitrage should be your routine. For me, it's habit. I have employees involved in every aspect of my business, but only my key managers are privy to what I consider to be the most important information. I take tasks and spread them over various groups. I have VA work groups that handle Facebook, groups that handle LinkedIn, groups that handle phone calls, and groups that handle transcription.

Task arbitrage serves not only an information security function but also an employee retention function. If an employee understands every aspect of my business, I've created an incentive for that individual to go off on his own. In effect, I've created a competitor. So, even with my key managers and executive assistants, I spread proprietary information among several people. For example, earlier I mentioned L. J., my key executive assistant in the Philippines. L. J. handles lots of very important and proprietary tasks for me, but she doesn't do everything. I give some proprietary tasks to Kristin, my U.S. assistant, just as a safety measure. In this way, no single employee ever becomes too "in the know"—or indispensable.

The "Worst Case" Mentality

Worst case: could your well-trained employees run off with some of your secrets? Sure. Could they become your competitors? They could, but how many competitors do you already have? And what's one more competitor, really? Is the "worst case" possible? Yes. Is it probable? No. As you've probably already noticed, living the laptop lifestyle is not just about putting procedures into place to automate your business; it's also about attitude. Just as you have learned to keep the most important, business-building tasks for yourself and delegate the rest, you must learn to do the same with your thoughts.

Keep the productive; cast off the unproductive. If you're not used to thinking this way, it may take some practice, but it's worth the effort. Living the virtual lifestyle means putting systems into place to manage your employees and protect your interests to the greatest extent possible, given that you're dealing with fallible, unpredictable human beings, and then letting the rest go. It may sound a little like "wax on, wax off," but Mr. Miyagi was on to something. So was En Vogue when they sang, "Free your mind; the rest will follow." Only when you learn to "free your mind" will you truly be outsourcing smart.

SAMPLE DOCUMENTS

Company Policies — Full-Time Virtual Assistant

1. Commit yourself to a full-time work schedule according to your eight-hour per day Monday–Friday arrangement at time of hire.

2. You will be required to give us a working e-mail address and Skype name, and you will be required to use these as daily forms of communication during your working hours.

3. You will be required to use a daily time report to chart your tasks as assigned by your manager. You will be required to submit your daily time report at the end of each pay period by the date assigned by your manager in order to receive payment for that pay period.

4. Your pay is based on actual time worked. Your eight-hour workday does *not* include lunch and breaks, or holiday or sick pay. You must log out of your time sheet for lunch breaks and log back in when you return. We allow for a one-hour lunch break during your workday.

5. If you wish to take more time off than one hour during your workday, or if you want to take days off for any reason, you will need to contact your manager for authorization and record this as time with *no* pay (unless you have arranged with your manager to make up the hours missed).

6. If you are sick or you lose Internet connection, you will need to contact your manager as soon as possible to report the reason for your absence. This will be recorded as time with *no* pay (unless you have arranged with your manager to make up the hours missed).

7. Per your contract, if you have a pay period in which you report *less* than or *more* than the regular full-time eight hours per day, your pay will be calculated by the hour per your work-for-hire agreement.

8. Pay periods are twice monthly, running from the first through the fifteenth and from the sixteenth through the last day of the month.

9. Any changes in your schedule, either temporary or permanent, must be requested in advance and authorized by your manager.

10. Per your manager's instructions, you will follow log-in procedures at the beginning of each workday and fill in your daily time report for tasks during the day.

11. You must always be reachable by e-mail and other instant messaging systems during work hours, per your manager's instructions (unless you're away from your desk for lunch).

12. If you have a question about your task, need clarification on the instructions for the task, or are having difficulties completing it, you must contact your manager immediately for further details and instructions. Do *not* proceed on guesswork.

13. At the beginning of your workday, review your tasks; if you do not have enough tasks for the day, notify your manager immediately so that you can be provided with more tasks. It is your responsibility to ensure that you have enough tasks to occupy your work hours.

14. You are not, under any circumstances, allowed to work for other clients or companies during your work hours for us. Please remember that you have signed a contract designating your hours and schedule.

15. Remember, per our work-for-hire agreement, which you have signed, that you will under no circumstances share our company documents or materials or software with anyone or use these documents, materials, or software for personal use.

16. You will be issued a warning for not showing up for work on time, not completing your tasks on time, or not being reachable during work hours. If this behavior continues after the warning has been issued, you may be terminated at the discretion of your manager.

Work for Hire Agreement

A Work for Hire Agreement is used by companies who outsource tasks to a person not in their employ: a VA, copywriter, social media manager, etc. It's a document under which a service provider agrees to provide services described in the form.

The person you outsource tasks to is an independent contractor and not an employee of your Company. This Agreement should not be used if the Service Provider is really an employee of your Company.

To put it simply, the Work for Hire Agreement is simply a short-form version of a Consulting Agreement. It should be signed by both you and your VA. The agreement becomes effective as of the date cited, usually at the beginning of the agreement. Once you design it, it wouldn't hurt to have your attorney review your form.

Sample Work for Hire Agreement

This agreement is effective as of: _____, between
_____ of, _____
and _____, of, _____.
Beginning on (date), the following services will be performed:
_____
_____
_____

Payment for Services:
Describe agreed payment amount and details of pay schedule

Termination:
This agreement shall be terminated automatically on _____.

Relationship:
It is understood that _____ *is an independent contractor with respect to* _____ *and not an employee of* _____.
No benefits, fringe benefits or insurance, etc. are being offered to _____, *nor will be supplied by* _____.

Ownership:

Any and all copyrightable material, patents, products or information developed in whole or part by _____ in connection with services provided during contract period, shall be the exclusive property of _____. If asked to sign documents to this end, _____, agrees to do so.

Confidentiality:

_____ agrees not at any time or any manner, either directly or indirectly, use for personal benefit, share, divulge, disclose or communicate information or property of _____. Strictest confidentiality is agreed and expected beyond, if and when, such a time that work agreement has been terminated. All notes, documents and records are sole property of _____.

Signature of (Company Name) Date

Signature of (Service Provider) Date

Virtual Assistant Time Sheet

Although, for various reasons, it's sometimes not advocated by many VAs, time tracking is an important component of outsourcing to a VA. Clients are only billed for time actually spent on tasks. Because of this, it's vital that a virtual assistant have some sort of system in place to track time. Some have their own forms. In case you're working with one who does not, here's a sample you can work with. As always, modify to your specific business.

Some outsourcers prefer to see the exact breakdown of their VA's time, while others aren't really concerned with it. Still, it's good business practice, especially when beginning a relationship, to have (and use) a time tracker that allows you to be aware of the breakdown, regardless.

Using an excel spreadsheet will allow you to label columns according to the information you'd like to have. There are also templates you can download. Depending on how much you need to micromanage, you'll decide on what you need to know. A word to the wise: most VAs are fiercely independent. That's why they became VAs to begin with. They may not take kindly to micromanagement. Unless you feel that you need one, a time tracker may not be necessary.

Since the VA is an independent contractor, you will not be concerned with breaks or lunch breaks. The VA will make her own schedule, unless time is a factor in performing the task.

Sample Time Tracker

Date	Log-in	Log-out	Log-in	Log-out	Total Hours
Monday					
Tuesday					
Wednesday					
Thursday					
Friday					
Saturday					

Total Number of Hours _____

Signature of VA: _____

Date: _____

No Pass Performance Review — Termination

Dear _____,

This notice is to inform you that your services are no longer required by _____ (or the _____ company). Per your contract with us, we are providing this as your three-day notice of termination, effective on this date, _____.

Reason for Termination:

Lack of following requirements for daily communication
Lack of proper notification for missed work hours
Unreachable during required work periods
Late or incomplete tasks turned in
Tardiness to work

Description and Examples:

1. _____

2. _____

3. _____

There are no further tasks assigned to you at this time. Please submit your daily time report as required at the end of our pay period on _____. This will be your final payment.

Per your work-for-hire agreement with us, you must return any documents, materials, or software in your possession belonging to us. Please also return any documentation of log-ins you possess at this time. Please be advised that as of the date of your termination, _____, you will no longer have authorization for access to these log-ins.

If you have any questions regarding this notice of termination, please contact us.

Regards,

_____ for

_____, owner,

_____

Pass Performance Review

Dear _____,

Per your work-for-hire agreement, your performance review for _____ month period is now due.

Any status and/or pay raise is based on the results of this performance review and the recommendations made by your manager and authorization made by the owner.

First of all, we would like to recognize your overall terrific performance. You started with us as a _____ and have continued to develop your skills at different tasks to achieve a high level of understanding and perfection.

Here are notes on your performance:

- Attends check-in procedures as required

- Completes daily time report and submits on time

- Fulfills all requested tasks to best of ability

- Pays attention to detail

- Provides short turnaround time

- Provides high level of support

- Goes above and beyond job requirements

- Asks for further tasks when finished with daily tasks

- Is a great team player and is willing to help others on the team

We also recognize that you are always ready and willing to work on whatever assignment you are given, even if it is outside of your comfort zone. You have had no difficulties adjusting to policies we have established for team members.

We appreciate your hard work and attentiveness to your tasks. At this time we would like to offer you a pay raise to $_____. This raise will go into effect as of _____ and will be reflected in your paycheck for the pay period ending _____.

Thank you for your diligence and the reliable support you offer this team and this company!

Regards,

_____ for

_____, owner,

_____

Performance Warning

Dear _____,

Your manager, _____, has recently expressed concerns regarding your work.

His/her notes indicate that your completion time on a recent client project did not meet expectations. Also, on multiple occasions, he/she has been unable to reach you during the workday.

At this point, we are issuing a warning regarding your performance. Your manager would like to establish specific guidelines to address these issues. We will review your progress by the end of our next pay period on _____.

Please contact _____ to let him/her know you have received this warning and to ask any questions you may have concerning your review date on _____.

For a traffic-generating, business building, outsourcing tip go to http://123Employee. com/outsourcesmart/interview/05, or scan this QR code and watch this video now.

THE MARKETING FUNNEL— OUTSOURCED LIST-BUILDING AND LEAD CREATION

6

If you enjoy list-building and lead generation, by all means keep doing it. But for most businesspeople, it's the most tedious aspect of marketing drudgery. There are many ways that new technologies and VAs can take over these tasks and, in the process, make your business exponentially more profitable. These strategies apply not only to generic businesses looking for more customers to buy their products but also to specialty and service industries, such as commercial building contractors or attorney services, that may not need exposure to the general public but do need name recognition within a specific industry.

THE MARKETING FUNNEL

Why are so many people still struggling to make money on the Internet? Some were oversold on the idea that it's easy. They expected to pick up some software that would generate a ton of leads and a ton of money. But to make money, you need to know how to attract traffic. You need a strategy.

As with any marketing task, the first thing you need to decide is whether to keep this task or delegate it. You have some options.

- Become a marketing expert.

- Hire a marketing expert.

- Find a business partner who is a marketing expert.

- Learn just enough about marketing to train an outsourced VA.

If you choose to work with a managed facility, your VA will know marketing, but she won't know your business. So you're not completely off the hook. You'll need to provide your VA with information about your business and your client base. Although there are infinite ways to create a marketing funnel, the process breaks down into three phases:

1. Attract traffic to your site.

2. Convert traffic to sales.

3. Convert leads into followers and fans.

Here are some of the most important aspects of a marketing funnel.

Attract Traffic to Your Site

There are many ways to attract eyes to your site. Pay-per-click ads are a popular method, but how many impressions actually result in sales? If you go with the traditional ad-sell format, your click-through rate is probably pretty dismal. In a marketing funnel, we want to think in terms of building relationships—and that building process begins with your ad.

Give Before You Receive

Does your ad tell customers what they can *buy*, or what they can *have*? Ads leading to information rather than to an immediate request for payment ultimately result in greater sales. So give tips and usable information to clients as the first step in building a relationship.

Opt-in

I talk about opt-in in more depth in the e-commerce section. When you add an opt-in box to your website, your marketing funnel has begun, and so has your relationship with the client. Capturing information about every visitor to your website means you have more than one chance to make a sale and that you haven't "lost" a customer who leaves your site. If you have every visitor's name and e-mail address, you can continue the relationship even if the visitor leaves your website without making a purchase. If you have their phone numbers, you can contact them right away. Consider offering incentives for contact information—a free gift for a phone number, another gift for a home address, which allows you to direct mail them as well.

The Ethical Bribe

Coupons and discounts are a tried and true way to attract traffic, especially for businesses that offer a service. Of course, you can offer the traditional "Get 20 percent off your next service at . . ." type of deal, but you can also create group-activated coupons following the very successful Groupon model. You can create a coupon that becomes activated when a specified number of website visitors click "like" on it. This is a great way to get people to share the coupon with their entire social network. You can also offer discounts to past customers who offer your coupon on their Facebook profiles or other social media pages.

But be careful. A friend of mine offered a discount coupon without an expiration date. The cost of honoring the coupon year after year almost put him out of business. Don't offer your product or service at or below cost unless it generates enough volume to result in profit. If you're not profiting, your site traffic will hurt rather than help you.

Up-sell

If a visitor to your site purchases one product, say, an online class for $189, an automated up-sell could then offer something else—perhaps a set of books to accompany the class—for a $79 up-sell.

Down-sell

If a visitor says no to the online class for $189, an automated down-sell might take the form of an exit pop-up that says, "We're sorry to see you go. . . ." At this point, you might offer a less expensive version of the class—perhaps a workbook—for a $47 down-sell.

Continuity Programs

If your website provides information that can be updated periodically, you can offer access to that continually useful information in the form of a membership. You might offer customers a $99 lifetime membership, or you might promote it as a monthly membership and charge $30 per month.

Once you've set up your funnel, you're continuously selling and list-building. You can sell to that list again and again, and those prospects become clients, who become fans. Then, when you sell them other people's offers, they become affiliates, and eventually they can become your outside sales force. If you've automated the funnel setup and management, your participation is minimal—and then you're truly living the laptop lifestyle!

Joint Ventures

The most powerful way to build your list is through joint ventures and affiliate networks. By partnering with others in related or compatible businesses, you can trade lists and pump your marketing out to all of their contacts. This reciprocal arrangement builds the businesses of all affiliates.

YouTube Marketing

We've all seen YouTube videos that have "gone viral": a goat on a trampoline, a cat riding a Roomba. It's usually something funny, useful, controversial, or amazing—and it gets millions of views. Do you ever see one of those things and think, "If only the YouTube video I made about my business could get a fraction of those views"? Unfortunately, business videos don't really go viral, but you can link your business's video to a viral video.

Here's how: Look for a video that's gone viral, one you can spoof. For example, my business partner and I recently created a spoof of the "Charlie Bit My Finger" video. Shoot it, and then attach the same keywords as the original. If you do this, your video will appear on the same page as the original. Some of the viewers of the original will view your spoof, and if you're lucky, your video will go viral as well. Your outsourced VA can put your video on your website, send it out on the video RSS feeds to increase your views, then back-link it to your website where the viewer will become a customer.

You can also create incentives for your website visitors to view your YouTube video by holding contests. If you offer points for every time someone "likes" or reposts your video—with the person who earns the most points winning a prize—you're spreading your marketing across many social networks and connecting with people who may not find you otherwise. Posting your contest in gaming rooms is particularly effective because gamers tend to repost. Even if they're not your target audience, they'll help you spread the word. Giving away a sought-after item, such as an iPad or camera, is an effective way to get people talking about your business and sharing your information with their networks. There's great software for these contests. I like Contest Burner.

SOCIAL MEDIA

Nielsen Report Spring 2012

The social media stats in the Nielson advertising report for spring 2012 surprised a few people. Go to http://www.nielsen.com/us/en.html to read the whole report.

According to the report, women are more likely to use social media than men. They're more likely than men to have blogs and Facebook profiles. When you're planning your social media marketing, consider that women are 18 percent more likely than the baseline American to follow a brand on Facebook or other social media sites while men are 21 percent less likely.

I find this fascinating. It's a known fact that women usually hold the purse strings. Smart marketers are aware of this. When it comes to certain products, they know just who to market to, but the Nielsen report shows not only that this trend translates to digital shopping, but that women are also more likely to be online in the first place.

What does this mean for you? It means, now more than ever, you need to have a sound social media marketing plan, not only if your niche is women, but if it includes potential clients of both genders. Developing and executing such a plan can be a full-time job, and there's no way you can do it by yourself if you're going to run your business effectively. I'd play the outsource card if I were you.

We'll talk more about the potential for social media to build your business later, but for now, let's just talk about how it can help with lead generation. This is one of the ways an outsourced VA can play an important role. A VA can set up Twitter and Facebook accounts devoted to your business and generate weekly or even daily content. As we discussed above, the "give before you receive" rule applies. Your tweets and status reports should be informative and aimed at interesting and helping rather than selling to potential clients.

Delegating social media is possible, but you need to know your role. You need to be the manager while your VA is the implementer. Your VA can post videos, quotes, and pictures, add friends, manage your inbox, set up events, post to groups, and add notes. But be careful about delegating your status updates. Your social network can tell when the content isn't really coming from you, and they'll tune out if it's too impersonal.

One day per week, you should plan your status updates and tweets and deliver them to your VA to distribute over the course of the week. I usually prewrite about 50 status updates and tweets for the week, and my VA uses Hootsuite.com to schedule them. It's a good habit to check in on your social media accounts every once in a while and respond to feedback personally. One option, though, is to text your VA throughout the day and let her know what you're up to.

At VegaInvestmentSolutions.com, Victor Vega Jr.'s VA helps with his social media marketing:

My VA has been phenomenal. She handles all of my social media marketing, my e-mail marketing, and she even takes my inbound phone calls. She is doing an amazing job. My staff loves her; she's easy to work with, and she's a hard worker. I was at a seminar once, and I checked my e-mail; in just a few hours, I had 143 Twitter followers following my e-mails.

Casey Eberhart, known as "The Ideal Networker," is a trainer who travels the world. He runs his entire business by outsourcing to VAs:

I got to tell you, before we got involved in outsourcing, some of our scheduling and inbound and outbound calls and our social media—it was all completely disorganized and messy. About six months ago, my Twitter account had a couple of thousand followers. As of today, I'm at about 20,000. My outsourced VAs are friendly; they're fantastic. They get done what they say they're going to do. I highly, highly recommend using a VA to take care of the tasks you may not be the best at or you may not like to do.

There are highly qualified VAs prepared to manage your social media marketing. How much time would you free up by outsourcing this task? (Author's note: by the way, at the time of this writing, Casey is up to 100,000 followers!)

Facebook Brand Pages

Created by Mark Zuckerberg and a few college friends, Facebook was launched in 2004 as a social networking site for Harvard University students before being opened up to other Ivy League schools and, eventually, the public. Sit in a public place and listen to conversations for 10 minutes, and I guarantee you'll hear the word *Facebook* at least twice.

Facebook allows you to create your own profile page with information and pictures and to link to other people's pages by "friending." You can post updates as often as you like about aspects of your life, on your own pages and on friends' pages. You can also connect by clicking a "like" button to acknowledge a point or express agreement, or you can comment.

Facebook is meant to be used for social interaction, although lots of people also use Facebook for business. Entrepreneurs, nonprofit organizations, and huge corporations use Facebook to garner followers through "like" pages. They used to be called fan pages. People interested in organizations are able to connect with others of like mind, and the organizations can market their products and services.

Facebook has made the world a much smaller place. Members now have the ability to create and join groups. They can promote events worldwide. People with common interests connect from everywhere on the planet.

The Facebook pages that get the most activity are theme pages rather than brand name pages. Although it may be instinctual to name your Facebook page after your business, this is a mistake. Facebook users search by theme or topic; they're not searching for you unless you're a recognized brand. So create pages about what your customer is interested in. The page name should contain keywords about your region or topic, not your brand. Let's say you sell picket fences in Des Moines and your company name is "Wilson Brothers." Facebook customers doing a search for a picket fence in Des Moines will find your competitor, "Jonson Brothers," because they named their page "Des Moines Picket Fences."

Again, the "give before you receive" rule comes into play. Sure, your Facebook page will show the name and location of your business, but its primary content should not be about selling product. You might post a video about how to waterproof a wooden deck, information about various types of wood and how they wear in different climates, or links to forestry sites. By posting helpful, credible information, you're earning client trust, which will bolster both your reputation and ultimately your profits.

Twitter

Twitter is a social networking service, much like Facebook. The difference is in the form and frequency of interaction. "Twitter profiles are stripped down to the bare minimum. You get a screen name and a profile picture. "Tweets" are 140 character "micro-blogs" that may go out several times a day, whereas on Facebook, updates are much less frequent. The 140 character limit allows you to get to the point and convey what's on your mind at the moment.

Much like friending on Facebook, you can "follow" twitter feeds, receiving updates whenever someone you're following posts. Without the photo albums and personal information, Twitter is a much more impersonal social networking site than Facebook. But its simplicity and ease of use allow people to easily and quickly update feeds.

You can use Twitter for business, and many do. Since the "numbers game" pays off here too, your goal is to get as many followers as possible. Twitter etiquette suggests when people follow you, you follow back. If you want to increase your followers organically, you or your VA will need to put forth some effort, but once you reach a critical mass, things take off. The hardest thing is to get to 2,000. After that, it gets much easier.

The first thing you can do to expand your list of followers is to unfollow anyone who isn't following you. Use Twellow, Tweet Spinner, or Tweet Adder to help you identify these squatters. Sign into your account, search under "view non-mutuals," and when the list pops up, you'll know exactly who they are, and you can unfollow them. This will help balance your numbers of follows and followers, something Twitter likes.

Once you've cleaned up your existing account, search for topics and people in your industry and follow them. The tighter your niche, the higher the quality of your list and the higher the probability you can monetize Twitter. Use Telly (formerly Twitvid) and Twitpic to share photos and videos on Twitter in combination with frequent tweeting to market your business.

> ### POWER MOVE
> *Twitter & SEO*

LinkedIn

LinkedIn is a social networking site characterized by its professional theme. Like Facebook's friends and Twitter's followers, LinkedIn has *connections*. Your connections are contacts who provide details about their businesses, their credentials, and recommendations from those who've done business with them. LinkedIn is unique in that it retains not only a record of your direct connections but also of your connection's' connections (second cousins) and your connections' connections' connections (connections by marriage). The purpose of this professional web is to make it easier for you to make introductions and increase your own direct connections. You don't need to be a business owner to benefit. LinkedIn also allows users to post and apply for jobs, and that goes for those who want to seek outsourcing opportunities and providers. The connections network comes into play here as you can find a common link between the job poster and yourself. If you're on the hunt for work, it's not always what you know but who you know. This goes back to what I said about people wanting to help people. Expand the detail in your profile to 100 percent, and use your connections on LinkedIn to get your foot in the door.

LinkedIn is the most powerful way to connect business-to-business. To get the most out of LinkedIn's list-building and lead-generating potential, you've got to do more than just set up a profile page and add a few connections. Join and interact with groups. Post articles that lead members back to your website. Find the group that's discussing your business area and join the discussion, but remember the golden rule: give before you receive. Don't sell, contribute. Post content that is relevant and helpful. Then, in the course of the discussion, you might direct other members to your blog—which will direct them to your website.

Your goal is to add people from all three levels to your list—and this is a job for your outsourced VA. Your VA can message your first level connections and ask for connections to the second level—then ask the second level for third level connections. Through this method, the databases of everybody you connect with through LinkedIn become yours. Then, every so often, give your VA a task (e.g., to invite all of your first level connections to a promotional event).

> ### POWER MOVE
> *LinkedIn top-linked list*

Let's review.

How to Outsource Your Social Media

- Become familiar with the various platforms (Digg, LinkedIn, Twitter, Facebook, Flickr, Blogger, Google, YouTube, etc.).

- Choose platforms that will benefit your business.

- Create your strategy for each platform (e.g., prewrite status updates weekly).

- Know your role.

- Delegate tasks others can do for you.

> **POWER MOVE**
> SoKule allows you to post on
> 86 social media sites at once.

SOCIAL MEDIA ETIQUETTE

Yes, Facebook has its own etiquette. Not everyone exercises courtesy and good manners, but you'll be remembered for it if you don't, so do. Here are a few guidelines.

Don't Just Invite Randomly

Be strategic when you invite and accept friends or followers. Send a personalized friend request. Introduce yourself and state why you want to friend the other person if it's someone you don't know.

Get Involved

Just as in "real life," you need to give more than you get. Post helpful comments and links to resources, and compliment others *authentically*. Share personal information (within reason) about yourself, and be friendly.

Don't Be a Media-Hound

If you're overly promotional, you'll turn people off. People want to know more about you. It's okay to promote your products and services on occasion, but don't make that your main focus. Sending out an announcement of your special event is fine; inundating your friends' mailboxes with frequent promotional messages is not.

Write Back

When your friends comment on your posts, "like" the comment, or write a few words in response. Let them know you care about what they have to share.

Commenting

When you comment on a thread, don't ever, ever, ever try to reel people away and over to your wall or website. It's rude.

Posting Etiquette

Don't Act on Impulse

Emotions can run high! Before you post anything controversial, wait awhile. Then don't.

Put Yourself in the Other Guy's Shoes

Think about how your communication will be viewed if read out of context, perhaps by your child or an attorney—or the IRS. Oh yes, they're also on Facebook, along with your clients, prospects, and other people you may not want listening to what you have to say.

Phone a Friend

If you're not sure about something you want to post, ask for the feedback of someone you trust before you send it. Friends can be more objective—and point out anything edgy or offensive, passive aggressive, etc. You may not be aware of how your communication will sound to others.

Resist and Desist

It may be tempting to respond to or initiate inappropriate or off-color communication, but resist. Put your thoughts and feelings down on paper and respond privately. Also, post nothing about politics or religion. If you currently post this type of communication, stop now.

Here Come Da' Judge

If you're tempted to vent on Facebook or Twitter, be aware that things can get out of hand. Defamation of character, slander, and malicious intent can be viewed unfavorably by a judge in a court of law, and it may cause you problems.

Communication with real-life friends has more flexible boundaries; however, if your clients will see your posts, you may be better off leaving personal or emotionally charged content to private messaging. Or here's a novel idea: pick up the phone.

Meetup.com

Meetup.com is an easy and affordable way to list-build. For $75 per year, you can start and run a meeting on the topic of your choice. As organizer, you can set criteria for your members and schedule meetings at locations and times convenient to you. Again, you're going to "give before you receive" by offering information to group members. (Groups that are thinly veiled sales ploys die quickly.) Members become part of your list and can lead to affiliates and customers. Your VA can help plan meetings by finding books, articles, or other content for discussion and sharing.

Networking Events

What to do with all of those business cards you collect at networking events? If you have a scanner and an outsourced VA, those cards can be a lead-generating gold mine. We attend events to meet new people and to gain knowledge, right? If you're like some people, you come home with a pocket full of business cards, which you put on your desk, in a box, or wherever. The point is that's where they end up. Your intentions are good, but a month or so later, when you may not even remember some of the people you met or why you'd like to get to know them, you toss the cards. You might as well burn money.

Here's what I do: after every seminar, meeting, training convention, or other networking event where I've collected a pocketful of business cards, the first thing I do is scan them eight at a time. I send them to my VA, and she takes it from there, putting all of the contact information on a spreadsheet and using Infusionsoft to generate an e-mail right away. Those individuals immediately become part of my list, but they don't remain just names; my VA helps me turn them into real, active contacts by corresponding with them. She sets appointments and I takeover. It's like a tennis match.

One thing your VA can do to turn your business cards into connections is send "It was nice to meet you" greeting cards with a video or other media, or an invitation to join your social network—become a Facebook friend, Twitter follower, or website visitor. After these initial efforts, you'll strike up e-mail exchanges with several contacts, meet others for coffee, and some may even become affiliates or customers. You'd be surprised at what a little outreach effort can do. Would you have the time or desire to reach out and follow up with the holder of every business card on your own? Probably not. But with the help of a virtual assistant, it's easy.

For a traffic-generating, business building, outsourcing tip go to http://123Employee. com/outsourcesmart/interview/06, or scan this QR code and watch this video now.

OUTSOURCED WEBSITE CREATION AND MAINTENANCE

7

Every entrepreneur wants an eye-catching, profit-generating website. The most dynamic websites contain shopping cart options and visitor-friendly opt-in systems. Most important, successful websites are promoted through a system of back-links that includes blogs, videos, and social networks. Many business managers enjoy website design, but if it isn't your thing, both website creation and maintenance can be delegated to an outsourced virtual assistant.

E-COMMERCE

Generally, an *e* in front of a word (e-book, e-zine, e-mail) means electronic. E-commerce refers to the buying and selling of goods and services over the Internet. Virtual stores, online catalogues, and payment transfer sites are all examples. As people become more comfortable with providing their information over the Internet, online shopping is becoming more popular. It helps that processes are also being simplified.

You want numbers? According to Wikipedia, e-commerce and online retail sales in the United States are projected to reach $226 billion in 2012. That's an increase of 12 percent over 2011. How much of that figure are you responsible for?

Let me ask another question. How much of that figure would you like a piece of? I'm going to be blunt: if you don't have a way to capture sales directly from your website, you're missing out on potential revenue. How much? *A lot.*

This is one of those "yeah, I've gotta do this someday" tasks. People walk away from this massive opportunity for wealth generation simply because they're intimidated by the process of setting it up. You don't have to do the work! Do you have products to sell? Do you have services that can be sold to a virtual clientele? You could be up and running and making sales *in a day*! There are only two steps to get you going:

1. Pick up your phone.

2. Call your VA.

Shopping Carts

Hang on, don't take out your credit card yet. I know, just the mention of the word *shopping* makes some people salivate. An electronic shopping cart is a tool that allows people to make online purchases. Visit a few e-commerce websites and take a look. A few clicks take you to a page where you can input your information. You fill your basket, your total bill is tallied along with any shipping costs, and soon after, the postman shows up at your door with a package—or five. Yeah, it's very easy to spend when you're using plastic. If the marketer has been effective, he has struck an emotional chord; one of the criteria for closing the sale.

Often it doesn't matter whether your new customer is using euros, drachma, or dollars. With a major credit card, money spends and money buys. Disregard small-minded notions that your product or service would interest only those customers who fit a specific profile. E-commerce will often surprise you. I doubt if it matters to you if the new member of your negligee-of-the-month club is a woman or a 75-year-old man in Fiji. I'd send the first shipment out the next day with a welcome-to-the-club card.

Social Shopping

Social shopping is a slang phrase birthed by—you guessed it—social media. Shoppers share their purchases and information about products and services through social networks, often including links directly to websites. (Are you getting this?) One way businesses can tap into social shopping is through affiliate marketing. You provide a link to members of your database who then sell your products and services for you through their own networks. You cut them a check, they sell harder, and the cycle continues.

If you don't currently have products to sell, affiliate marketing can be a great way to generate revenue while you build your business. Here's one reason a large database is critical: your clients, followers, and friends become your outside sales force. They post on Facebook in niche groups, and some will even put your ad on their websites. Visitors click and immediately go to your site, where hopefully you have a system for capturing leads, and voila!

Your VA can do your affiliate marketing for you. It's easy. It just takes time. Once you see the checks start rolling in, you'll be hooked. Why would you not? Being a middleman is the least expensive way to generate income—no product development, no stocking, no cost for fulfillment; you just refer.

Exercise Caution

As you're selecting affiliate propositions, be sure you check out companies as thoroughly as possible before you begin recommending them. Your recommendations will reflect on your business, and if you recommend poor products and services, you could tarnish your reputation.

Opt-in Systems

One way to take advantage of leads generated by affiliate links and inbound links is to have an opt-in feature so you can market to these prospects in the future. It's also a good way to safeguard against being labeled a spammer for sending unsolicited bulk e-mail. By opting in, visitors give their permission to receive bulk e-mail. Newsletters and marketing pieces usually require an opt-in.

An unconfirmed opt-in runs the risk of being labeled spam when no steps are taken to confirm the authenticity of an e-mail subscriber. Typos in the address may also cause the e-mail to go to the wrong person. A confirmed opt-in (COI) is a request made by a subscriber, which is then authenticated by a test e-mail sent to the address provided by the subscriber. This test ensures that no one can subscribe another person in error or without the person's knowledge. This method, called a double opt-in, protects both you and your subscribers. An opt-out feature allows you to automatically put subscribers on your list and give them the option and ability to unsubscribe.

Obviously, these opt-in systems are tedious and require attention to detail (boring!). It's the detail, not the difficulty, that often keeps people from diving in headfirst. But hey, there's probably a VA who loves this kind of stuff and is just waiting for an opportunity to help. What do you think?

Back-links

This chapter wouldn't be complete without a discussion of back-links, one of the most vital building blocks to your online success. You've probably heard the word, but I want to be sure you understand what back-links are and why they're important.

Back-links, also called inbound links, are links to your website. If they fit certain criteria, they'll set you in good standing with the search engines. They offer a form of recognition and important feedback in a search query. The number of back-links you have indicates the status or popularity of your website. Google and other search engines will give more credence to your website if it has a good amount of quality back-links. The key word here is *quality*. Search engines consider those websites with quality back-links more relevant than others in a search.

What defines a quality back-link? First of all, random links don't do you a bit of good. Let's say you're in a category-protected networking group of 50 professionals, and each of you links to the other. Fifty back-links is a pretty substantial number, right? Not when it comes to search engines' qualifying standards. Don't waste your time. You won't impact your position in a search—unless back-linked sites have content related to your site. You can actually dilute your relevancy. I'll tell you why in a minute.

When you stand on common ground and share related content with inbound links, these inbound links are considered more relevant to your site. The higher the relevance of inbound links, the greater their quality.

When search engines calculate the relevance of a site to a keyword or key phrase, they consider the number of related inbound links. So don't be satisfied with merely collecting inbound links—focus on getting inbound links that share content similar to yours.

For example, if you're in the business of creating green cleaning products, and you receive a back-link from a website or blog that touts the benefits of green living, that would be more relevant in a search engine's assessment than a link from a site about automobile parts—unless the site's content highlights green automobile practices. The more relevant the site is that's linking back to your website, the better the quality of the back-link.

Back to reciprocal linking. A while ago, it became common for companies to scratch each other's backs by exchanging links. One company points a link on its website to another website, and vice versa. Those nasty search engines (enter Google) got wind of it and began to filter out these sorts of relationships. Many of the cross-links were not relevant and thus simply discounted. Furthermore, while the irrelevant back-link was ignored, the outbound links still got counted! The relevancy score of many websites was weakened, and some dropped off the Google radar altogether.

Still want to make it work with your networking group? Decide on some shared relevant content before you link. Shared doesn't mean duplicated. Use your imagination and come up with unique material.

Other Benefits of Back-linking

Achieving quality back-links will also help to boost your visibility. Traffic doesn't come naturally the day your website goes live. You have to get the word out. One way you can promote your website is through reciprocal linking. Keep in mind what I said earlier about reciprocal linking. Be very picky about who you link with. Make sure the website is likely to be deemed relevant by search engines.

Outsourcing Your Back-linking

Seeking out relevant web partners to back-link to is tedious. It takes time and patience. Another drawback is one many of us succumb to: our propensity to follow the little white rabbit that leads us deeper into the Internet when we discover something of interest. It's easy to lose focus on your search, especially when something else captures your attention.

By giving your VA the search criteria, she can locate relevant sites to link to and then handle the mechanics behind the scenes.

For a traffic-generating, business building, outsourcing tip go to http://123Employee. com/outsourcesmart/interview/07, or scan this QR code and watch this video now.

OUTSOURCED ARTICLE MARKETING AND BLOGGING

8

Most businesspeople associate article writing and maintaining a business blog with drudgery. But this task can be successfully handled by your choice of either outsourced virtual assistants or technology. Aggregation software like the former Article Marketing Automation (http://www.articlemarketing automation.com/) and blog networks such as WordPress, Blogger, and HubPages can automate the process.

Whether you choose to outsource this task to a virtual assistant or use the technology yourself (which, as you know by now, you shouldn't do), you'll need to understand the basics. Because of the huge number of article marketing and blogging training videos available online, the temptation for many busy entrepreneurs is simply to seat a virtual assistant in front of a video. However, like anything else connected with your business, you'll need to know enough about the process to be able to choose the right tools (e.g., article submission software)—even if you're not the one who will be using them.

PRODUCING E-ZINES AND
DRIVING TRAFFIC

I'll say it over and over because I can't say it enough: one of your most important goals is to drive traffic to your site. It's where people get to know you and, once they do, where they'll convert to clients or customers and buy your products or secure your services. You can make this happen. The strategies you're reading about in this book are going to help you.

Writing articles and circulating them will do part of the job, especially if you guest-blog. Visiting other virtual neighborhoods exposes you and your ideas to new people. If they want more, they follow you. Make them want more: be interesting, a bit elusive, and offer value when they stop by to visit your part of town. As long as you continue to offer value, you'll keep visitors long enough that they'll want to get to know you better.

Check with anyone who offers free workshops or seminars. Successful speakers always offer something of value to attract prospects—refreshments, free gifts, a glass of wine. Guests come for the bennies and end up buying. Especially if you serve wine.

You can do the same thing on your website. Free offers, mega-content, and opt-in VIP member offers draw traffic and encourage visitors to spend a little time with you. As I said, articles and guest-blogs are a great way to introduce your business to new people. Want to know an even better way?

E-zine marketing can be highly valuable. Keep sight of the word *marketing*. E-zines can serve as free gifts, be full of mega-content, and flood followers with valuable opportunities. That'll keep 'em coming. But traffic alone won't keep the lights on. Customers do. Be sure you also focus on making sales.

There are plenty of ways for you to buy clicks and up your traffic, but the best way to increase sales is to target high-quality traffic. Here's where your e-zine will help you hone in on your target market.

Before you let yourself feel that familiar sense of being overwhelmed that comes when you're already doing too much, remember, you can outsource the complete project to your VA. Read what Stephanie Hartman, founder of MITprograms.com (millionaires in training) has to say about how she outsourced a newsletter project. She actually made a huge profit by doing so:

> When I finally got around to e-mailing a newsletter to my clients, I wondered what I had gotten myself into. After the second one, I wished I had never started, but my clients were expecting it. It was actually a pretty good source of leads. A step at a time, I decided to delegate the project to my VA. Now she does the whole thing. She researches the subject matter, writes the articles, produces it, and sells ads. She covers her payment and makes money for my company on top of that. I forgot to mention that she also e-mails it— right on schedule, I might add! I don't know what I ever did without her.

Do your best to attract website visitors who know what you do and a little about what you sell. Your newsletter or e-zine will help make sure they're interested—or at least a little curious— and willing to buy! This is where your content comes in—keep thinking outsource.

If someone is going to spend time reading your e-zine, it'll be because they're clear about its value. It meets their needs on one or more levels. Offer value, target your audience, and meet their needs: they'll buy. Hang on a second. E-zines are great, but they aren't the complete answer to your marketing challenges. Pay attention to the other marketing information in this book as you plan. In the following section, I want to make sure you understand what an e-zine is and how it will work as a component of your marketing plan.

What Exactly Is an E-zine?

An electronic magazine (e-zine) is usually delivered by e-mail to a list of subscribers. You might receive an e-zine without requesting it if someone has added you to his database or if a friend shares it with you. If the publisher is doing his job, you might also receive links via social media.

E-zines are sometimes called newsletters. There's really no basic difference. If a newsletter is on the longer side, or if it contains a variety of elements, it might be best referred to as an e-zine.

E-zines are published daily, weekly, biweekly, monthly, or whenever the publisher feels like it. The most successful e-zines are delivered to a highly targeted niche of readers. These readers are interested in a particular subject and want to hear more, so as long as you don't badger them three times a day, they subscribe. No kidding. Some marketers really do this.

> ### POWER MOVE
> Which do you think yields the best results: daily, weekly, or monthly e-mails? The answer may surprise you. (See the end of this chapter for the answer.)

Your readers have two characteristics: they are interested in your product or service, and—after they read your brilliant content—they are inspired. Once inspired, they become motivated, and things really begin to happen. If you're a service provider, for example, you can build rapport with your readers by discussing how little time we have these days, how quickly technology is advancing, and how nice it would feel to have a little help—all of which will inspire them to consider options. Reminding your readers how easy it is to outsource will inspire them. Showing them how cost efficient it is will motivate them to take action.

Match your offer to an e-zine about things your target market would be interested in. You'll tap into a pool of followers eager to know more. Those who value good health want to know more about wellness. They read about the benefits and, when motivated, buy health-related products. People who feel overwhelmed will buy a book that gives them, say, five secrets to stress relief. Businesspeople who want to be successful in today's marketplace buy websites, social media services, leads, autoresponders, and anything else that will take them to the next level. You bought this book, right?

E-zine marketing encourages people in your niche to visit your website. When they get there, they'll have the opportunity to buy or to sign up for more information. You can buy ads in other people's e-zines, or you can sell ads in yours. You can also submit the articles you've either written or outsourced to others.

You can build your list and make sales through joint ventures with other people in your industry. For instance, you can make an arrangement with an e-zine publisher or associate to e-mail your offer, with an endorsement, to her list. This costs you nothing unless you make a sale, in which case you open your wallet and share the revenue with her based on what you've negotiated in advance. Some joint ventures are 50/50, some are 80/20, and some are 100/0—in favor of the host. That's an indication of how valuable your database is, so if you haven't started collecting yet, start now.

Your e-zine can be completely outsourced—from the research, to the writing, to the design and distribution. In fact, as an affiliate, you don't even need to sell your own products. Link with Amazon, ClickBank, web hosting companies, and a variety of other products and services, and you'll receive a regular check without expending an ounce of energy, except maybe to run to the bank—which you can also outsource, by the way.

WHY USE ARTICLE MARKETING TO PROMOTE YOUR BUSINESS?

Article marketing is the third most effective way to promote your website, second only to joint ventures and Google AdWords. Because article marketing is viral in nature, your articles—with their back-links to your website—spread far and wide. Once you write an article, other business owners copy it, with info about the author (you) intact, and publish it on their websites. When you create usable content that is easily found in a keyword search, customers find you, trust you, and go to your website to find out more about you.

In a nutshell, the benefits of article marketing include:

- Establishing you as an expert in your field or niche

- Promoting a relationship of trust with your customer-readers

Article-Writing Phobia

Writing can be intimidating. But don't let bad memories of your eleventh-grade English teacher make you phobic about article marketing. The articles you'll be writing are short and factual—and they won't be graded by a middle-aged teacher holding a ruler and dictionary.

Who Should Write the Articles?

Ideally, you should write your own articles. But how do you know if you're a good enough writer to get picked up by the article submission sites? One way to test your writing ability is to write an article and submit it to a couple of article submission sites, like EzineArticles (http://ezinearticles.com/) and Buzzle (http://www.buzzle.com/). If your article is accepted, you have the skill to write your own articles. If not, you might have grammar or usage issues and be better off delegating this task.

Reasons for Outsourcing Your Article Writing

You may want to delegate your article writing if:

- You don't have the English skills to write a clear, grammar- and usage-error-free article.

- You have the ability to write a great article, but you need hundreds of articles written in a short amount of time.

- You just don't have the time.

FINDING A GOOD GHOSTWRITER

Finding a ghostwriter is easy. Finding a good one is hard. A common mistake is looking for a bargain-basement ghostwriter. In most cases, the writer with the cheapest rate is the one with the worst skills. It's up to you: if you want a bargain, you typically need to hire someone who doesn't speak or write English fluently. This may be worthwhile (e.g., if you don't mind doing a grammar clean-up after each project).

Ghostwriters can be found at the following freelance sites:

- https://www.elance.com/

- http://www.vworker.com/

- https://www.mturk.com/

- http://www.writingandtranscriptionservices.com/

- http://www.craigslist.org/

The most popular of these are probably Elance and Craigslist. Craigslist will usually result in a better rate, but it can take longer to find someone because of the many separate regional databases. Another disadvantage to Craigslist is that there's no customer feedback system. The advantage is that you can judge writers according to the quality of their classified ads—which they've penned. That's a writing sample *not* available on Elance.

Go to one of these sites, and post an ad. Be clear and specific about your needs. Your ad might say, "I need 10 articles on the subject of _____, by _____ date, using these keywords: _____." Before you hire a candidate, get a writing sample. It's also important to choose a writer with a history of positive ratings from other clients. Another safety tip: award your project to multiple writers, and see which one produces the best work. Then work only with that person in the future.

What You Should Expect to Pay

A reasonable rate for a quality writer is $8 to $10 for a 300- to 400-word article. Need an Article (http://needanarticle.com/) charges $5 to $7 per article. Expect to pay a deposit (one-third to one-half of the total fee) to a writer you've never worked with before. But once you establish a working relationship with a writer, usually no deposit will be expected on subsequent projects.

Life is easier for everyone if you set up a routine with your content writer. Have her write a set number of articles per week, so the pay is regular. Paying a content writer via PayPal is easy and provides a record of each transaction.

Watch Out for Plagiarism!

After your ghostwriter submits her first article, make sure it has not been plagiarized. Article directories will not accept articles that have been copied from elsewhere online. You can use Copyscape (http://www.copyscape.com/) to search for duplicate content on the Web. If Copyscape finds duplication, it will show you the web page on which the document was found and how many words it has in common with your text. The cost is five cents per search.

You can do a manual search by copying a few words of your article's text and then pasting them into a Google search box. If that exact phrase comes up on a search result, your ghostwriter may have plagiarized. You should not pay anyone for plagiarized work, nor should you hire that person in the future. Also, if you found your ghost plagiarizer on a site that allows for customer feedback, you can warn future customers by giving a rating of "unsatisfactory" or by specifying details.

For people who want the benefits of article marketing without the work, WeSubmitArticles (http://wesubmitarticles.com/) will write articles and submit to article directories for you.

THE THREE PARTS OF AN ARTICLE

A marketing article consists of three primary parts:

- Title
- Content
- Resource box (aka bio box)

Let's look at each of these parts in more detail.

The Title of Your Article

The title is the most important part of your article. It's what will prompt a potential customer to read or ignore your article. Your title should grab web surfers' interest by offering a benefit. It should entice them to click on the link in your resource box.

A good title:

- Is interesting

- States how the article will benefit the reader

- Is clear and easy to understand

- Contains keywords that match and will lead back to your website

Unfortunately, most article marketers pay attention only to the "contains keywords" part. Yes, your two or three main keywords should appear in your title. And yes, a keyword-rich title will make a search engine like Google send readers to your article. But you're writing for human beings, not just search engines. A list of keywords is not an article. To be successful at article marketing, you have to remember the human part.

Choosing a Human Being–Friendly Title

Although search engines "read" articles based on keywords, if you want to engage human beings, your article must have an interesting title. A title like "Home Buying" may contain your keywords, but let's face it—it's not all that interesting. A title like "I Bought a Money Pit" is interesting but doesn't contain your keywords. You want to find a middle ground, such as the title "Don't Buy a Home That's a Money Pit." Remember, you want to do two things, write a title that's keyword-rich *and* interesting to human beings.

The Dash Is Your Friend

If you're having trouble thinking of a title, a dash can save you. Let's say your article is about tax preparation. You want your title to include the keyword phrase "tax preparation," but you know that's never going to attract human readers. One option might be: "Tax Preparation—How to Avoid Getting Ripped Off." Now you've got keywords for the search engine and a little bit of interest for the human beings.

Numbers in Your Title

Studies show that people are drawn to odd rather than even numbers. Also, if you're using a number in your title, use the number (7) not the word (seven). Hey, the human eye wants what it wants!

The Content of Your Article

Your article should be a problem-solver. It might discuss a problem in your industry, propose a solution to a problem, offer a list of frequently asked questions, or provide instructions for how to do some task or find some product or service. It should fill a need.

Body

The body of your article should be divided into at least three paragraphs. Avoid paragraphs of only one sentence—unless that sentence should stand out for effect. The opening paragraph should give the reader an idea of what the article will cover. Make a statement or ask a question in your topic sentence, then support or answer it in the body of the article. Each paragraph should lead to the next paragraph—you want the reader to reach that resource box at the bottom of the page.

Conclusion

Your final paragraph should summarize what has been stated in the body. After that comes the resource box with info about you, the author, and a link to your website. Finally, let readers know they can reprint your article as long as it remains intact and includes the resource box.

Content Rules

There are three important rules to follow concerning the content of your article:

1. **No Links!** Your article should not contain any links to your website. Most article directories won't accept an article with self-promoting links in the body of the article. However, you can have links to neutral sites such as Wikipedia.

2. **No Ads!** Article directories won't take an article that looks like an advertisement. It should be fact-based and helpful to a reader who is looking for information about how to do something or do something better. No advertorials.

3. **Use Keywords!** If your site is about car insurance, use the phrase *car insurance*, and use it several times throughout the article. But be careful that your use of keywords seems natural. Using keywords in the body of your article will improve its ranking.

How Long Does It Have to Be?

This is probably the question you asked your high school English teacher every time he assigned an essay for homework. And he probably answered: "As long as it takes to make it *good*." I don't know about you, but I always hated that answer. Never fear: the question "How long does an online marketing article have to be" actually has an answer. It should be between 300 and 600 words. An article shorter than 300 words isn't informational enough and won't be taken seriously. Most e-zine publishers won't publish it because it's not likely to be of much value to readers. As for the upper word limit, reasonable minds differ. Some say 600 words; others say 750. Who's right? Typically, e-zine publishers don't publish long articles. And since you want e-zine publishers to pick up your article and publish it, you should keep it under 750 words.

Around 400 to 600 words is optimal. That works out to about seven or eight paragraphs. How long is a paragraph, you ask? Typically, a paragraph is three to five sentences. But again, you're not being graded. Contemporary writing allows for one or two sentences, and a paragraph can also be something as simple as a bulleted list.

The goal is to be informational without giving everything away. Remember, the ultimate goal is to direct readers to your website, where they'll find more info. If they feel like they have enough info, you'll defeat your own purpose.

The Resource Box

A resource box (also called the author's bio, bio box, or about the author) is a paragraph (between two and five lines) at the end of the article with information about you, the author, and a link (or links) to your website for more information. It should not contain exaggeration or a salesy tone.

A resource box might be formatted something like this:

To learn more about (topic) _____, visit my website (link) _____. You can also find out (link) how to paint a house at my website.

Below the resource box, type a statement giving others the right to reprint your article without a fee as long as the article is not changed and the resource box remains intact. This will make your article more mobile.

Information About the Author

You might also include information about you, the author, such as how you acquired your expertise on the article's topic. For example: "John Doe has been practicing law for the past 20 years. He specializes in real estate law and publishes a weekly newsletter for real estate agents. You can learn more about real estate law at Doe's Real Estate Today, http://www.doereales-tateadvice.com."

The web address must be written as http://www.doereales-tate.com rather than just www.doerealestate.com. This makes it a clickable link rather than just a copy-and-paste web address.

Recap: What Goes in the Resource Box?

- Your name

- Your background

- What makes you an expert in the field

- An offer of something free (e.g., newsletter)

- A link to your website for more info

Change It Up

Your VA should change the format of your resource box every time you submit your article. Why? If you submit your article to 10 different article directories with the same resource box, Google will begin to ignore the links in your resource box. It will be seen as spam. If you vary the format and wording of your resource box, it seems more natural. Remember, search engines are looking for naturally occurring links—so that's what you want to mimic. Think about how links occur naturally: someone sees a useful website and puts a link to it on his page. Sometimes a link will read "click here," but other times it will be a keyword phrase. To mimic this type of natural linking, ask your VA to vary the text in your resource box.

SUBMITTING YOUR ARTICLES

There are two ways to submit articles: (1) through article submission sites, and (2) through manual submission to websites.

Using Article Submission Sites

One of the most popular article submission sites is Unique Article Wizard (http://www.uniquearticlewizard.com/). After your VA writes your article, she can submit it to all of the article directories for you.

But before you submit to Unique Article Wizard, you'll need to rewrite the article two more times, with two more (different) titles. Why create three unique versions of the same article? Because search engines like unique content. If you submit the same article to 1,000 directories, it will be rejected, so be sure your VA is on top of this. Unique Article Wizard helps you turn one article into many slightly different, unique articles by rearranging the paragraphs for you. Their online training walks you (or the VA you've delegated this task to) through the process, step-by-step. The downside of using Unique Article Wizard is that it doesn't change the resource box, which you or your VA will need to do so that your article isn't perceived as spam.

Submitting Manually

If your VA submits your articles manually, it's important for her to remember to change your resource box for every three to five sites. Also, make sure you read the submission specifications for each site, since they have different formatting requirements.

To get the most out of submitting articles manually, follow this four-step plan:

1. Submit the first version of your article to EzineArticles. Make sure your content is original.

2. Submit the second version to a few other directories.

3. Put the third version on your own website or blog.

4. Keep a list. You'll receive an e-mail from every site that has approved your article. Keep a list of these sites so you can link to those articles in the future.

Article Marketing Sites

http://www.Ezinearticles.com/   http://www.goarticles.com/

http://www.articledashboard.com/   http://www.expertarticles.com/

http://www.articlebiz.com/   http://worldvillage.com/

http://www.articlecity.com/   http://www.buzzle.com/

http://www.articleblast.com/

EzineArticles will award you "Expert Author" status if they accept and publish your articles. This status can be displayed as an icon on your website or blog.

Categories

If your VA is submitting manually, each site will ask her to choose a category where your article would best fit. This can be difficult because your article won't be accepted unless you pick a relevant category. Choose a category that's not too specific but not too broad. For example, if you've written an article about cancer, choose the cancer category and not the health care category. But don't go too specific, either. If your article is about cats, it would probably not be accepted into a category about Siamese cats. When in doubt, err on the side of going broader than your topic. If your article is about diet foods, health or weight might be acceptable categories, even if the site doesn't have a diet category.

HOW ARTICLES HELP YOUR RANKING

Search engines (like Google) love articles. After all, it's articles that come up as the results of a keyword search—not advertisements. When web surfers type keywords into a search engine and your article comes up in the search results, in theory they'll read the article, then click on the link to your website in the resource box. When Google sees those clicks, it increases your ranking.

Every time a reader clicks on a link in your article, which leads back to your website, that click acts like a "vote" for your website. And, in the world of search engine optimization, the website with the most votes wins the rankings race. Remember, the more places that link to your website, the better Google thinks your website is. Articles can improve your website's incoming links, which improves your ranking.

The best part: since most article directories are considered "authority sites," having your articles there will move you up in the rankings even more dramatically.

Frequency

How often should you submit articles? For the best results, you should submit an article about your website at least once per week.

Consistency

Consistent article marketing will ensure that your site's incoming links continue to increase. For best results, you want a steady, constant increase in incoming links. Why? Because slow growth is read by search engines as more legitimate, and sites that grow at a slow or moderate pace are considered to be more valuable and are rewarded with higher rankings.

Google and the other search engines know what's natural. If you never get any links to your site and then suddenly get 500 links overnight because you submitted an article via Unique Article Wizard, Google will discount those links as "unnatural," and those links won't affect your ranking. So you must submit articles regularly, rather than in spurts.

Recency

Search engines don't want to deliver stale search results to their users, so they consider the recency of links to your site. If you stop submitting articles, you're telling the search engines that your website is no longer relevant. If you keep submitting articles, however, the older links will help you. Search engines value links with a long life span—when they're linking to a site that's still getting fresh links.

Common Article Marketing Mistakes

- Content that reads like an advertisement (advertorials)

- Content that is not useful

- Content that is not entertaining

HOW TO FIND KEYWORDS

What keywords should you include in your articles? The obvious answer is: include keywords that are being searched for most frequently. There are many tools for determining possible keywords. Here are just a few.

Wordtracker

Wordtracker (https://www.freekeywords.wordtracker.com/), a web-based keyword research tool, is both helpful and free. When you submit a topic, Wordtracker's "keyword suggestion tool" offers 100 keyword phrases related to that topic.

Google AdWords

Like Wordtracker, Google AdWords (https://adwords.google. com/select/keywordtoolexternal) is free and returns a list of keyword phrases related to your topic. But Google's keyword tool also lets you know how much competition you have for a given keyword. This allows you to choose keywords with high search volume but low-to-moderate competition.

Paid Keyword Search Tools

Paid keyword tools include Keyword Elite (http://www.keywordelite.com/) and NicheBOT (http://www.nichebot.com/).

Keyword Elite

In Keyword Elite, after you enter a keyword, you can choose which search engines (e.g., http://Ask.com/) you'd like results from. You can also choose the number of keywords to be returned, up to 10,000. A "competition" column lets you know how many of your competitors are also targeting your keywords. As with Google AdWords, you'll want to choose keywords with high search volume (popular words and phrases) but low-to-moderate competition.

WHERE TO FIND ARTICLE CONTENT

- **Online magazines.** Go to http://www.magazines.com/ to find a huge selection of magazines.

- **Bookstores.** Visit a local bookstore and skim magazines for information.

- **Niche magazine.** Buy a subscription to one of the most popular magazines in your field.

- **Trade magazines.** They're usually free to professionals.

- **EzineArticles.** An article directory site. "Search" by entering a keyword or phrase. A long list of articles containing your keyword phrase will appear. Look at the type of articles most popular in your niche (e.g., reviews, tips, how-to, etc.).

- **Google search.** Do a search and skim the first few results for interesting article content. Highlight aspects you like about each article. Then have your VA use these as models for your articles. You or your VA can rewrite them in your voice, add some of your content and transitions, and there's your article.

- **Yahoo groups.** Enter your keyword, search through Yahoo's public forums, and look for common themes and hot topics.

Private Label Rights (PLR) Articles

These are bulk articles about a single subject, sold in a package. Once you buy them, you can submit them as is or alter them. To submit a PLR article you've rewritten, make sure it's perceived as original content by the search engines. Problem: you're not the only one buying these articles. If you use PLR articles, make them your own by doing a total rewrite or just tweaking a few words here and there. Change titles and subtitles completely, but make sure the title still reflects the article's content. Replace words in titles with synonyms. If articles contain links, replace them with your own affiliate links or with links to products you choose that relate to your content.

Drawbacks to PLR Articles

- Some of the articles are well written, and some are not, so don't use them without proofreading!

- Search engines look for spam, and some of the articles may contain duplicate material.

- It's best to use PLR articles only to inspire ideas.

Sources for PLR Articles

- http://www.plrpro.com/

- http://www.contentgoldmine.com/

Using EzineArticles to Write a Keyword-Rich Article

One way to write a keyword-rich article is to use EzineArticles as a brainstorming tool. Go to EzineArticles and peruse the existing articles about your topic. Copy small sections of text you find interesting from one article. Then do the same with another article. Reword, reorganize, and insert original content to create a unique article. Remember your optimal word count of 400 to 600 words.

Writing Articles with "Instant Article Wizard" (IAW) Software

After a little practice, you'll be able to use Instant Article Wizard to create an article in less than 30 minutes. The software walks you (or your outsourced virtual assistant) through the process, but the basic steps are as follows:

1. Choose your topic (and up to three subtopics).

2. Let IAW search for content. At this stage, IAW searches the Internet, collecting "short copy chunks" from various websites. It copies only one or two sentences from each site to avoid duplicate content.

3. Rearrange. Now you can organize these found chunks of text in any order you prefer.

4. Select the chunks of text you will use for the intro and conclusion.

5. Clean up. Edit your article by inserting paragraph breaks and transitions.

Keyword Density

Articles should be keyword-rich so search engines will notice them and deliver them as results. The keyword density equals the number of times your keyword appears related to the overall length of an article. Optimal keyword density is 1 to 3 percent. To determine your article's keyword density, go to http://www .live-keyword-analysis.com/. This site checks your keyword density—for free.

Article Submission Outlets

Many outlets are looking for quality articles. They need content, and you need back-links to your site. By having your VA submit your articles, you're allowing these outlets to use them in their e-zines, blogs, or websites, as long as they include your resource box. Just some of these outlets:

- **Article directories** (Most are free and are considered "authority sites" by the search engines.)

- **E-zine publishers**

- Blog publishers

- Website publishers

Software

"Article Submitter" ($40 to $50) is a program that helps you submit articles. You can submit an article to 25 directories in 30 minutes or less. You could easily outsource this task.

"Article Assistant" and "Article Submitter" are basically the same software with different graphics.

Outsourcing Article Submissions

If you decide to outsource your article submission process, you can hire an individual or use a service.

YOUR ARTICLE MARKETING PLAN — THE BIG PICTURE

Before you start feeling overwhelmed with details and procedures, let's remember that article marketing consists of only five steps:

1. Write articles.

2. Upload articles to your site and/or blog once or twice per week.

3. Submit articles to article directories.

4. Submit articles to magazine or newspaper publishers in your industry.

5. Watch the magic. If your articles are interesting, they'll be picked up by your affiliates' sites and blogs, and by many article directories. If your articles are interesting *and* well written, they'll be picked up by e-zine publishers, blog publishers, and website publishers.

Dealing with Affiliates

If you have affiliates, send them your articles. They're always looking for content.

Article Directory Sites

There are hundreds of article directory sites, and the list changes all the time. As of this printing, here are just some:

http://www.365Articles.com/

http://www.ArticleBar.com/

http://www.GoArticles.com/

http://www.Buzzle.com/

http://www.PromotionWorld
.com/

http://www.ISnare.com/

http://www.ArticleDashboard.com/

http://www.Add-Articles.com/

http://www.ArticleCity.com/

http://www.ArticleHub.org/

http://www.EzineArticles.com/

http://www.SubmitYourNewArticle
.com/

http://www.Constant-Content.com/

FORMATTING ARTICLES

Most article directories accept only articles that meet the following format requirements:

- No more than 60 characters per line

- No word processing formatting

- No hard line breaks after each sentence (only between paragraphs)

A free downloadable software program, NoteTab (http://www.notetab.com/) can help you format your articles. This program strips out hidden Word formatting. It also shows you the frequency of every word in your article. This is a good way to check your keyword density.

TO CHECK BACK-LINKS

Marketleap (http://www.marketleap.com/) tells you the number of back-links created by your articles and where it found them (e.g., Google, MSN, or Yahoo!).

DISADVANTAGES OF ARTICLE MARKETING

- You need writing skills or the willingness and funds to hire a ghostwriter.

- Even if you have a flair for writing, writing articles yourself can be time-consuming.

- Submitting articles is time-consuming. It can take a full day to submit to a large number of sites. Outsource it!

ADVANTAGES OF ARTICLE MARKETING

The advantages outweigh the disadvantages; article marketing is an investment that will continue to pay out over time.

- Free (unless you pay to have someone write articles for you)

- Effective (creates a large network of back-links in a short amount of time, which helps you boost your search engine ranking)

- Viral (one article creates back-links, increased traffic, and credibility)

THE KEY TO WRITING EFFECTIVE ARTICLES

The key is to provide interesting, usable info without revealing everything in your articles. You want to lead your reader to the rest of the information—which is available on your website. The point is to establish yourself as an expert in the field. Selling should be done at the website and never in the article.

Remember to Proofread

Just because you've finished a rough draft doesn't mean you've created a masterpiece—or even something entirely readable. A good practice is to put your article away for 24 hours before reading it over. Even better: get a fresh pair of eyes on it. Ask a friend to read it and give objective feedback. Did they stop reading at any point? Where? Odds are, that stopping point contains weak writing and should be revised.

SEVEN TYPES OF ARTICLES

There are seven basic types of articles. Some writers prefer to stay with one type, but varying your format is a better way to go. Remember: we're all about unique, fresh content here. The seven types of articles are the tips article, the story article, the personal experience article, the facts article, the recommendation article, a review of products or services, and frequently asked questions (FAQ). Let's look at each one in detail:

1. **Tips article.** This article does just what you'd think: it gives tips on a topic, such as how to lose weight or how to choose a dentist. Tips might be formatted as numbered (or alphabetic) lists or listed with bullets. How many tips? A good rule of thumb: don't exceed 10 tips. Most

importantly: include the number of tips in your article's title (e.g., "10 Tips to Help You Lose That Post-Holiday Bulge").

2. **Story article.** This type of article tells a story—usually about a problem and how it was overcome. The solution should lead the reader to your product or service. Your story can be true or fictional and is usually written in third person. (If you write a story about your own experience, it falls into the next category, the personal experience article.) The important thing is that it should be entertaining enough to keep readers engaged all the way to the end of the story—where they will find your resource box.

3. **Personal experience article.** In this article, you'll recount a personal experience that somehow relates to your product, service, or your industry in general (e.g., "How I Made My First Million in Real Estate").

4. **Facts article.** This type of article is research-based. It provides the reader with interesting and/or useful information in the form of concrete facts or statistics. For example, an article entitled "How Mold Affects Your Body" will be based on medical, scientific, and/or anecdotal evidence.

5. **Recommendation article.** This must be informative even though it's used to promote a product or service. You may be recommending a certain brand of cleaner, but the article can't sound like a sales pitch. Show that one product does something others don't do—and remember to keep it factual.

6. **Review of product or service.** Simply review a product or service related to your niche market. This works particularly well with affiliate marketing.

7. **Frequently asked questions (FAQ).** These articles address any possible objections a target customer might have to the writer's product or service. They also offer answers to overcome those objections. To find out what these questions might be, visit discussion forums about your type of product or service. There you'll find the most common customer complaints and concerns your articles could address. For example: "Does product ABC come with a guarantee?" Write the answer in an objective, un-salesy tone. For example: "Yes, product ABC comes with a two-year guarantee." Stop there. Gushing or bragging will take away all of your credibility.

8. **Combination article.** Okay, I know—I said there were seven, but realistically, you're often going to combine types. For example, your article might be part personal story and part fact, such as ending a recommendation with a personal story. If you combine types, be careful that your article isn't longer than 750 words.

> **POWER MOVE**
>
> SAQ article: should ask questions!

APPEAL TO DIFFERENT LEARNING STYLES

You're putting a lot of effort into writing your articles and circulating them. I'm sure you want to get the most mileage out of your efforts—and dollars if you're outsourcing. People take in information in different ways, so be sure your articles appeal to the greatest variety of readers by keeping in mind the different learning styles.

Just as there are different communication styles, there are different types of learners. Some people are visual learners. They understand concepts by seeing them, and they love to read. If they want to remember something, they write it down. When they see it, they can call it forward in their visual memory. Auditory learners remember what they hear—like every word to a song or people's names. Kinesthetic learners are touchy-feely people. We all learn through each of our senses, but one is usually dominant.

Count on your readers having different learning styles. If you want to reach them, you'll be most successful by including elements that will be picked up by the greatest majority. If you want to sell products or services, this is even more important.

When we write, we do so with our dominant learning style. If you're not paying attention to creating a "sensual" experience for readers by touching on all of the senses, your articles will appeal only to those who share your learning style.

Go ahead and write your article without scrutinizing it closely, but before you publish it, ask yourself if it will appeal to those with other learning styles. If not, add in a few sensory details.

ARTICLE WRITING TIPS

- **The first draft is for content.** In the first draft, don't worry about spelling, grammar, or usage errors. Focus on the ideas only. Save the editing until after you've got your basic content down.

- **When it's time to edit, do it carefully.** Put your article away for a day or so before picking it up to edit. Time gives you perspective. It also helps to get another, more objective pair of eyes on it. Don't submit your article until you've corrected all of the grammar and usage errors. Even basic errors can reduce your credibility and alienate your reader.

- **Respond to a need or answer a question.** Look at your article from a customer's point of view. What are your customers' questions? What are their concerns? Visit customer forums to learn about their questions and concerns.

- **Leave 'em wanting more.** Write until you've said *almost* all you want to say. End slightly before the end—so that your reader will want to click on your link to get the rest.

- **Stay on topic.** It's easy to go off on tangents. If you find yourself going astray, try writing an outline first, and stick to it.

- **Be clear.** Many writers lapse into pretentious language out of insecurity. Don't use any words in your article that your reader would have to look up in the dictionary. Write like you speak, and don't use verbose jargon.

- **No sales pitches allowed!** Avoid *salesy* language, exaggeration, and "sales hype." Turning your article into an advertisement is a turnoff!

- **Be original.** Don't plagiarize. Write your own article, in your own words, about your own personal experiences. If you quote a source, cite it.

USING INTERVIEWS

Interviewing experts in your subject area is a great way to add credible content to your articles. You don't want to simply transcribe an interview and use it verbatim. Instead, choose interesting tidbits from the interview. It's also interesting to begin or end your article with quotes from experts.

Make sure to attribute! Provide a mini-bio about the expert somewhere in the article. If the person you interviewed will be unknown to most readers, give facts about how she is qualified to talk about this particular subject.

You don't have to be a professional stenographer to use interviews. This is another task that can be easily and affordably delegated. Transcriptionists can be found online.

Be sure to prepare for your interview beforehand. Make a list of questions. What insights or tips can this expert share with readers? What pitfalls has she encountered and overcome?

ARTICLES VERSUS ADVERTORIALS

You may decide you want to advertise in a magazine or e-zine. Here's a tool that'll increase your probability for success in reaching your target market. It's the only time you're allowed to be a little "salesy."

Advertorials are a creative way to disguise advertisements. Tread lightly here. Never publish advertorials as blog posts or on Facebook, and never try to pass them off as articles. Use them only as they are intended: for the purpose of advertising in print media.

The advertorial demands a different tone than a typical informational article. At the same time, it needs to be more creative than straight advertising copy. The challenge is to switch from an obvious promotional article to something more "newsy." Writing advertorials can be tricky even for copywriters, so unless you're confident in your skills, outsource the task to a professional writer. During the interview process, be sure you ask to see samples of advertorials your job candidates have written before you hire.

If you know what you're doing, most readers won't even realize they're reading an advertorial until they're deep into the copy.

But let's start at the beginning. What is an advertorial? According to Wikipedia:

An advertorial is an advertisement written in the form of an objective article, and presented in a printed publication—usually designed to look like a legitimate and independent news story. The term "advertorial" is a portmanteau of "advertisement" and "editorial." Merriam-Webster dates the origin of the word to 1946.

In other words, an advertorial is an advertisement written to appear as editorial matter. It captures readers' interest by providing value, something that also makes it blend in with the other articles in the publication. The reason advertorials work is that people tend to gloss over printed ads just like they ignore banner ads and display ads. Because they look and sound like the other articles, they fly under the radar. Readers are drawn in.

As with all articles, you'll need to have an attention-grabbing title, and your advertorial will be laid out like editorial content in the publication, with maybe a picture or two. Your copy will be written in an "inverted pyramid" style, a common method for writing news stories. The copy leads with the most important or interesting information.

Even though advertorials may seem outdated, print isn't dead yet. More and more offline copywriting techniques are being used online. Just as advertorials have worked in print, they'll work online.

Now, back to our Power Move question from earlier in this chapter: should you e-mail daily, weekly, or monthly? What do you think? The answer is, *daily*! I told you you'd be surprised.

The most successful marketers e-mail daily. Does this mean you should e-mail daily? No. You decide. The frequency should reflect you and your company's public persona. We e-mail weekly at our companies, but we do a lot of promotions, so sometimes it feels like daily. Experiment. Only you know for sure.

For a traffic-generating, business building, outsourcing tip go to http://123Employee. com/outsourcesmart/interview/08, or scan this QR code and watch this video now.

OUTSOURCED
VIDEO MARKETING

9

How are you doing so far? I know there's a lot to think about. But don't just think. *Act.* Even if you never dreamt there was so much to running a business, remember, you don't have to do it by yourself. Your trained VA is an invaluable resource if you take advantage of outsourcing. Video marketing is an area many avoid because of its complexity. It's a mistake I hope you don't make. Between you and your VA, you can manage it. Once your system is in place, it almost runs itself. The rewards are astronomical.

This chapter will explain the benefits of video marketing and provide a concrete, how-to approach. I've outlined the differences between the various video-sharing platforms, including YouTube, Vimeo, Twitvid, and uQast, and I've explained the importance and method of creating back-links.

Finally, I'm going to walk you through the process of automating video submission services, so that maintaining an ongoing video presence—a powerful marketing strategy—takes no more than a few minutes per month. By delegating the creation and dissemination of videos to a VA, you'll be able to go back to business as usual.

VIDEO SUBMISSION: STEP BY STEP

Before we break down each step of the process, let's look at the big picture.

1. Create a video.

2. Choose the correct format. Each video site has a preferred format. In most cases, you'll save your file in wmv, avi, mov, or mpg format. Don't save your video as an swf—that's a flash file.

3. Upload. In Traffic Geyser, you'll upload the video before you start the submission process; in others, it's the opposite.

4. Input description. Insert the appropriate description, keywords, and tags for your video.

5. Watch the magic. Most video submission sites will submit your video to between 50 and 100 different video sites.

Create videos and submit them. Take advantage of the traffic YouTube gets—create videos users want to watch. If not, at least create a video with links.

Automating Video Submission Services

When done appropriately, video is a powerful marketing strategy, right? The goal is to be creative enough to get others to share your videos with their networks, thereby becoming your *virtual sales force*. Posting in as many places as possible increases the likelihood that you'll connect with your virtual sales force, and being imaginative ensures they'll want to share.

Posting your videos on Facebook will give you only so much marketing mileage. Using a video submission service will help you get onto as many sites as possible and also help you with the process of maintaining an ongoing video presence. It's pretty easy and literally takes no more than a few minutes a month.

Video marketing has become a major force online, not only because it's richer in media bandwidth, but, thanks to its entertainment value, it leaves other forms of marketing choking in the dust. Videos provide interactive marketing of your products and services. The more you post or get others to do so, the better you become at playing the age-old numbers game associated with making sales. Distributing your videos by way of video-sharing sites can quickly build quality incoming one-way links, which, as you'll remember, helps boost the SEO rankings of your site as well as filtering direct traffic from these sites.

Choosing the Best Service

You'll be best served by working with an experienced video submissions service. Sure, you could outsource the job to your high school sophomore, and he will probably be able to circulate some of your video material, but if you're going to take video marketing seriously, it's best to work with a company that knows what it's doing. Make sure whomever you use knows how to optimize your video with suitable titles, meta tags, and descriptions. You'll want your videos SEO-friendly before submission by experienced video submitters.

Some services do every submission manually. Others produce automated submissions. As long as your videos have complete SEO optimization prior to being distributed to top video sharing sites, you're on the right track.

Video Submission Tips

When submitting videos to submission sites, there are a few things you'll want to take into consideration. First, it's best to do a little research within your niche. How are your peers putting out their videos? What's the competition up to? Is there anything special you notice about the videos of industry leaders? It's a good idea to look closely at everything they do and the way they do it. They're the ones with the budget to afford high-level marketing advice, so you'll benefit from modeling their efforts.

As often as you can, try to use main keywords as tags or keywords—whichever is required by the submission site. Pay attention to specific tags used within your niche. Suggestions for other videos you may want to watch are based on videos with the same tags.

Remember, there are more videos online than your prospects have time to watch. If you want to stay in the game, you'll have to capture their interest quickly by using creative descriptions and titles that get attention. Again, model yourself after the heavy-lifters in your industry. They've hired professional writers whose job it is to make sure they get noticed.

If it works, use your URL as the title. Vary your titles; attractive, keyword-rich titles engage viewers and prompt them to click. Once they're watching, they're likely to stick with you if you've done your job creating a good video.

Want a little secret that will increase the probability that other videos you've produced will get a little play after someone sees one? When you're finished watching a video on YouTube, you've seen the way similar links are displayed, ready for you to click. Well, if you include in your keywords a code word that's unique only to you, something no one but you knows, all your videos with that same keyword embedded will come up as click suggestions!

Here's an example. Let's say you use the name of a popular actor in the title of a video. Of course, you'll also have listed his name as a keyword, right? So your video comes up as one of the choices for this actor. Someone clicks on it—because you have an *interesting* title, right again? When the video finishes playing, the available suggestions that pop up are not videos about the actor but *your* videos containing *your* keywords. And because most people have short attention spans, they sometimes forget why they were watching the other video and click on another one of yours—you know, one with an *interesting* title. It's easy to go off on tangents when you're watching YouTube. This *really* works.

Let's summarize a few things about video marketing, and then I want to discuss two specific video submission sites. First, I think we agree that video marketing is not only one of the hottest marketing trends but that it's essential for ranking on Google and the other search engines. Second, by using video submission tools, you'll save time and increase Google dominance on searches. Third, different submission tools can produce different results. And fourth, you can make things even easier by outsourcing your video submissions to a trained VA.

The submission sites Traffic Geyser and TubeMogul are similar, but with different benefits, so you'll want to use both. Although they offer good instructions for use, the process is kind of complicated, and don't bother writing them down because—*surprise*—they change often.

For each submission site, you'll have to create an account. Record all of those user names and passwords. They'll store the user names and passwords for you. Just input them into their system.

Traffic Geyser

Traffic Geyser (http://www.trafficgeyser.net/) is a membership-based tool that saves time you would have to spend submitting to all of the directories on your own. You upload once only. Traffic Geyser automates the task of content distribution so that you can focus on content creation. One of the primary reasons people use Traffic Geyser is to increase Google dominance as videos perform well in Google searches. In fact, search results using your keywords can improve while using Traffic Geyser. Annual subscription plans are available, and if cash flow is an issue, you can get a monthly subscription to Traffic Geyser for under $50. Check it out.

TubeMogul

Cash flow *really* tight? Consider TubeMogul (http://www.tube mogul.com/). It used to be free, but it's still inexpensive, and you don't need an account for everything. As with Traffic Geyser, you'll save time. TubeMogul will connect you with a highly targeted audience, and it tracks billions of video streams every month from the Internet's top publishers. It'll help you hone in on consumers who want to watch your videos—and they'll watch them longer.

As you can see, there are benefits to both Traffic Geyser and TubeMogul. If you decide to upload yourself instead of outsourcing, it'll take a little time to learn. Honestly, why bother when you can have your VA upload for you?

Submit videos about every week, and, if possible, make sure that your URL shows at the bottom of every video throughout the whole video. If this is not possible, make sure you put it in at least one frame at the beginning and end. This will help direct traffic immediately to your website and also increase opportunities for back-links.

Pinterest

There's another social media platform you may want to consider adding to your marketing mix. It's an "online bulletin board" called Pinterest (http://pinterest.com/), and it's quickly gaining in popularity. Pinterest is not going to be right for every business, but depending on your business and your Internet marketing plan, you may be able to use it to your benefit. By the way, don't feel you have to add everything into your social media marketing that comes along, but if something makes sense, it's worth a try. I'll give you a little background. See what you think.

Most Internet marketers agree that the fewer clicks required by your visitors to get to the information or product they want, the higher your conversion rates will be. To get to your website, Pinterest requires just two clicks after a visitor first sees something of interest. If Internet marketers are right, that translates into more leads, and, if you're content is on point, more sales.

For example, let's say you have a software program for sale. You pin an image from your sales page to your board. When one of your followers clicks on your pin, it'll allow him to share it immediately. If he clicks it a second time, it'll take him to the site the image was originally pinned from—in this case, the sales page for your software program.

Because Pinterest has such a large following, it's a great tool for driving more traffic to your site. It does this via links attached to the pins you place on your board. Believe it or not, tracking stats show that Pinterest is driving more traffic back to websites than Facebook or Google+.

Every pin includes a link leading back to the source of the image, making it simple for your followers to share your pins and link back to your site. This can translate into more inbound links to your website. That's another reason to build your database and increase your number of followers. The more followers you have, the more those followers share your pins, and the more traffic is driven to your site.

You can connect Pinterest with your Facebook profile and with Twitter, so your pins are automatically tweeted. And you can add a "pin it" button to your website the same way you do with other share buttons, so your visitors can pin for you. As I said, it's not for everyone, especially if you're already so overwhelmed that you're not doing justice to your other social media marketing. But if you think Pinterest sounds like something you'd like, outsource the task to a VA who specializes in this expanding network.

VIDEO MARKETING

ABM is an acronym familiar to most successful entrepreneurs: always be marketing. It's the key to notoriety and profitability in the marketplace. There are a lot of ways to market your products and services. Among these methods, the most cost-effective has got to be the Internet. Through web channels, social media platforms, blogging, and other tools we've discussed—provided you bring a solid product line and/or quality service offerings to the table—the Internet provides a flexible, inexpensive vehicle to prosperity. With the right moves in place, the Internet can help build your database as your business attains large-scale visibility, and a database is the currency of the twenty-first century (i.e., *ka-ching!*).

That being said, possibly the most effective of all online marketing strategies is video marketing. If you're not living under a rock, you've surely noticed the use of online video, in both personal and professional contexts. Almost everyone has a phone with video capability, and if they don't, they usually have a flip cam, a hand-held device about the same size as a cell phone. Just look around next time you're at a show or theme park. It's actually pretty funny.

No doubt about it, video marketing is the hottest trend to date in the marketing industry. E-mail and text marketing have their place, but the impact made by video marketing far exceeds both of these combined.

Here's why. It's always better to show than tell. Can't get more visual than with video!

Now, don't get me wrong. Every form of marketing has its place. But video marketing engages people like no other medium, and we've just scratched the surface.

In case you're not familiar with the concept of marketing, I'd like to spend a little time introducing you to it. That way, when I go into more detail, you'll know what I'm talking about. Sound good? Great!

Let's start by defining it and briefly discussing the difference between two things that are often confused: marketing and promotion.

Marketing takes into account the big picture: Is your product or service suitable for your target market? How are the quality and value as related to need? Is your price competitive? Are you lower in cost than your competitors? Better quality?

Promotion is only one aspect of marketing. It's made up of two major components, push and pull marketing, both of which are necessary. Push marketing involves getting potential distribution associates or joint venture partners interested in helping you market. Pull marketing is targeted toward your potential audience; it's what you do once your distribution channels are set up (e.g., Internet, radio, TV, print advertising) so they will buy what you're selling.

Back to video marketing. Once you determine what you're selling, how much you're charging, and where you'll sell it, your videos will help you promote. If I'm taking you into unfamiliar territory, don't worry. Before you finish this chapter, I'm going to tell you everything you need to know about using video to market your business—and I'm going to tell you how you can outsource most of it.

How to Use Video Marketing Effectively

Video submission helps to build your brand. People are generally more likely to click on a video link than they are to read an article, especially if you build a reputation for producing quality videos. They become familiar with your brand, and once they get to know you, they're likely to do business with you in the future. The more you pop up, the more deeply your brand becomes ingrained. It's a proven fact that the political candidates with the biggest signs (or small signs pounded into the ground in the most places) often receive the most votes.

Your video is your sign. The more places you can post it, the more it supports your overall marketing strategy. Here are some tips on how you can maximize the value of video marketing for your business.

Posting Your Videos

So, you've made your videos. Great! Where are you going to post them? There are many choices available to you. Some work better than others, but you really can't post in too many places. Building partnerships with other businesspeople and posting for each other using social media platforms with an endorsement or referral is a good way to build your database with people you may not have met otherwise.

Your Website

Place your videos on your website to draw interest and provide additional site content. Do you belong to any online communities? Posting video clips in such places will offer more visibility. People will get to know you more easily. In fact, don't be surprised if you run into people who seem to know you—people you don't remember. Using video is a powerful way to build relationships.

Online Blogs

Videos posted in online blogs should be short and sweet. They might include updates, news, and special promotions. Inform your viewers about the latest news, and entice your audience to click on the link to your site for more details.

For video blogging sites such as a few of those listed below, your goal is to get people to share and repost your video. Be entertaining and creative, and always include your URL. Your products can be featured, but your videos must never be a straight sales pitch. You're never going to be referred or reposted that way. Viral: that's the goal.

There are differences between the various video-sharing platforms. I'll discuss each one briefly before we talk about how you can manage your own campaign.

YouTube

I don't think there's anyone over the age of four who hasn't heard of YouTube, which was founded in February 2005. Billions of people watch and share original videos. YouTube is used by both amateur filmmakers and advertisers as a distribution platform for original content. Some videos become so popular they attract tens of thousands—even hundreds of thousands—of views in days or weeks.

Keep in mind, Google owns YouTube, so they favor it. Any video you create should be posted on YouTube. When you or someone else shares the link, and people click on it, they have access to all of your videos. Just make sure you include a common keyword, unique to you, every time you post, and your videos will be available to viewers.

Vimeo

Here's something fun. Vimeo is a community that focuses on people getting to know people. When you find videos you like, leave comments. Let the people who posted them know what you think about their videos and why you like them. Or, just as you would on Facebook, click the "like" button. Once you connect, they're likely to check out your videos. If they comment on or "like" your clips, their contacts will have access to your videos, which will help increase the number of views your clips receive.

Twitvid

Twitvid is pretty simple. You can log in with your Twitter account and share your videos. You just upload and then tweet. Oh, make sure you know what you're tweeting—Twitvid has a feature that allows real-time uploads, which lets followers actually watch the video while you're uploading it from your cell phone or webcam. Imagine how great this would be for viral video marketing. You could quickly tweet the video and ask others to retweet.

uQast

If you're an expert in your field, an author, or an Internet marketer, you might want to look at uQast as part of your video marketing campaign. Through this fast-growing online media supersite, you'll be able to set up your own online store. It also comes with a built in shopping cart and credit card processing. What if you don't have your own products? With a sound affiliate marketing plan, you really don't need them. Other companies pay you to promote and sell their products. Through uQast you can connect with these companies and make money selling thousands of digital products (and I know it sounds like a cliché, but it's true) while you sleep, play tennis, cook dinner, or whatever.

All of these video-sharing platforms are people-friendly, but unless you're really into micromanaging, they'd probably end up on your task list—meaning what? They can be easily outsourced to a trained VA.

VIDEO CREATION

When prospective clients hear *and* see your message communicated in multimedia videos, they're more likely to remember you.

Seeing and hearing a message at the same time increases memory retention by over 80 percent.

Creating video can be as simple as using raw footage from your own flip cam videos, or you can take it a step further and use video production software. There are times when raw footage works best to build rapport with your audience. For instance, when using testimonials to promote events or endorse products, credibility is best achieved with raw footage. You might edit (fade out, etc.) for brevity, but there's nothing like an authentic vote of approval from someone you're sure is a "real person" and not an actor.

There are, however, creative ways to produce entertaining videos that will engage the viewer. The longer they watch, the more time you have to win them over.

Animoto

Animoto was founded in part by former producers from MTV, VH1, Comedy Central, and ABC, who incorporated production skills they honed while working in television. The application produces online content comparable to what you'd see on television.

Animoto (http://animoto.com/) incorporates your photos, video clips, and music to generate video footage. You'd think with over a million people using the site to produce their videos in more than 150 countries, they'd spit out a bunch of cookie-cutter clips and everything would look the same. But the company strongly asserts that no two videos are ever the same.

Create short and sweet video clips or feature-length videos, or create video products with a white label option. White labeling allows you to sell the rights to your content to a company that will put its own label on it. Do you think every soap company manufactures its own detergent? No way. Many companies—in any industry—buy product at wholesale prices and slap their own name on the bottle.

Refine your content, customize your videos with your brand, and take it to market. I've said it before, but it bears repeating: ka-ching!

Screen Shot Videos

So, you're camera shy? You like the idea of creating video, you just don't want to be on camera. Screen shot videos are a great way to reap the benefits of video marketing and to produce demonstrations without having to pucker up for the camera.

A screen shot (also known as a screen dump, screen cap, screen grab, or print screen) is an image taken from a computer monitor. It's usually a digital image taken by software running on the computer, but it can also be captured by a camera or another device.

If you teach teleseminars or webinars, or if you want to circulate videos to promote your business, screen shots can be used to demonstrate just about anything. Like video, they're visual, interactive, and can be quite creative.

Camtasia

Camtasia Studio and Camtasia for Mac are screen video capture software that come with a free trial, so there's no risk. Try it before you buy it. Prior to recording, you define the area of the screen you want to capture. Camtasia Studio also allows you to record audio from a microphone or speakers and to place a webcam's video footage on the screen. Even if you're just learning, you can produce professional-looking videos in three simple steps: (1) record, (2) edit, and (3) post online. Screen shots or screen casts are perfect for showcasing new products, orienting clients, and teaching customers how to use your product. You can record PowerPoint presentations, webinars, and software demos, and it's relatively inexpensive.

Screencast

Not every video campaign is meant for a public audience. Sometimes you want only to reach private viewers with your video content. With Screencast (http://www.screencast.com/) you can control the level of privacy when you share your Camtasia videos online. It's a great avenue for academic professionals and other businesspeople seeking to manage and share videos, images, or documents. Screencast's high-quality content hosting offers you complete control over how, when, and to whom your content is distributed. You're the boss!

> **POWER MOVE**
> Check out Article Video Robot
> (http://www.articlevideorobot.com/).

Video Strategies

One thing we've learned about the Internet: nothing goes away. This is both good and not so good—especially if you have something to hide. Every video you make is a reflection on your business. Sometimes you've got just one chance to earn a new client, and a poorly produced video can forfeit that opportunity. It takes 10 times the energy to retrieve a lost opportunity to do business with someone than it does to earn their respect and admiration at your first point of contact.

Make sure every video you create is as high quality as possible. If it's not something you're proud of, delete it. This is not to say you need to be "perfect." Actually, slight imperfections make you seem more human. By quality, I'm referring to sound, clarity, and preparation. If you're filming outside, make sure the sights and sounds don't outshine your remarks. Determine in advance if anything is likely to surprise you, and compensate for possible distractions.

Whenever you're addressing an audience—whether live, via audio, or via video—preparation is key. Know what you want to say, communicate in a style that's respectful, and follow the guidelines in this section.

Most videos have people in them. Seeing faces elicits an emotional reaction, and viewers will watch more attentively. For videos targeting an English-speaking audience, if you (1) speak good English, (2) speak without saying "um" a lot, and (3) have a webcam, create videos with your face in them.

Since the second best thing to a face is a voice, write out a script or bullet points, then produce your videos using pictures. The most effective way is to record yourself with your webcam and also record the audio. If you don't have access to a webcam, just record audio. Never lose sight of the fact that your videos are a reflection on you and your business. If you don't speak English well enough, consider that there are lots of other ways to take advantage of video marketing.

Another way you can compensate is to write a script and record your video playing the text with music in the background, or with a combination of pictures and text. There are programs that can help you do this with little effort.

Some Ideas for Creating Videos

Use Windows Movie Maker—you can download it free. Windows Movie Maker is software that enables you to create videos and slide shows on your computer. You'll be able to design professional-looking titles, regardless of your experience. The program allows you to insert pictures and audio, and you can spice up your videos by creating transitions and effects. You can add music and even narration to give your videos a sleek, professional look and feel. When your video is ready, you can use Windows Movie Maker to publish and share.

Camtasia Studio allows you to record yourself talking through a Power Point presentation or to use music instead. You can record yourself going to a website for demonstration purposes. This is a great tool for teaching. Budget restrictions? No problem; there's a free alternative, CamStudio (http://camstudio. org/). It's not as good as Camtasia Studio, but you can certainly use it to record what you're doing on the screen.

Keep in mind, we're not talking feature-length films here. Your videos can be 30 seconds long. The point is to get traffic to your website. Simply present a challenge and promise to provide a solution at your website. Remember to follow through with any promise you make—no bait-and-switch. You'll shoot yourself down in less than the 30 seconds it takes for people to watch your video. Be authentic, give value, and give them a reason to keep coming back.

There's a lot to know and remember. Things are changing all the time. There are always new techniques, new tools, and innovative ideas being introduced. Hire a VA and stay abreast of video marketing, and you'll be exposed to the most contemporary concepts. Keep learning. It'll keep you fresh and one step ahead.

One thing should be top of mind: drive traffic to your website. On each site you decide to link to, you can make the profile page link back to your website. Users will watch your video, go to your profile, and then go to your website from there. The more traffic you have, the more visible you are to the masses, and the more opportunity you'll have to increase visibility. Once you garner a following (and as long as you keep their trust), you'll be able to monetize your efforts.

Video Submission Tips

- When submitting videos, try to use main keywords as tags or keywords—whichever is required.

- Look at videos in your niche—notice those tags. Suggestions for other videos you may want to watch are based on videos with the same tags.

- Try to use descriptions and titles that get attention. Also, use your URL as the title or at the beginning of the description.

- Vary titles.

> ### POWER MOVE
> Put your phone number in your URL.
> It works, and nobody does it!

For a traffic-generating, business building, outsourcing tip go to http://123Employee.com/outsourcesmart/interview/09, or scan this QR code and watch this video now.

OUTSOURCING THE GOOGLE-RANKING RACE

10

When most entrepreneurs think of Google rankings, they think of the struggle to find the right keywords and codes. But today, quicker and easier methods are available to take care of this task, and the maintenance of Google ranking, like the other tasks we've already discussed, can be delegated both to technology and to well-trained virtual assistants.

MANY TOOLS AT YOUR DISPOSAL

There are several ways to boost your business's Google ranking, from the strategic choice of your domain name to setting up back-links through social networks, blogs, video profiles, and social bookmarking. Tools at your disposal include deep linking, MaxBlogPress Ping Optimizer, yfrog, Metacafe, Dailymotion, Jumptags, and SocialBot. Also, RSS feed aggregators—including Feedage, RSSMicro, RSSBOT, and Nuerolinker—can help to automate it all.

Your Domain Name

Just as you probably spent some time choosing your business name, you should put a lot of thought into choosing your domain name. Your business name may not be vital to the success of your business (although we could argue that point), but your domain name is definitely vital to the success of your website when it comes to Google ranking.

At the most basic level, domain names are important because they act as your business or personal address on the Internet. Computers on the Internet have an Internet protocol (IP) address, a sequence of four numbers separated by periods, such as 456.789.1.0. Even if you were a genius, it would be nearly impossible to remember the IP addresses of all of the websites you visit. The domain name system was designed to assign a unique name to each IP address. Because they're word-based, they're much easier to remember.

But domain names are much more than just pneumonic devices. Registering a memorable domain name can mean the difference between a successful Web presence and floating around lost in cyberspace. The best case scenario would be to register your business name as your domain name. Companies with websites such as amazon.com, microsoft.com, or farmersinsurance.com don't have to worry that potential clients won't be able to find them online. If you're an independent contractor, try to pick up your name—John Smith.com—as a domain. It may not be available if another John Smith already owns it, but try to get it.

Your business name might be available to you even if someone already owns it. Cyber-real-estate investors purchase domain names with catchy phrases and high-profile words and then resell them. It might cost you $50 or $5,000, but you may be able to get the domain you want. The question then becomes: why would you pay big bucks for the right domain name? I'll tell you why.

Two aspects of your website speak loudly about your professionalism. The first is having a memorable domain name; the second is investing in a professional website. Both show potential customers that you're an established, legitimate business.

You could publish your site through a free web hosting site, but your URL will look something like www.xyz.com/-yourbiz. This address looks generic, and unless someone already knows you, will probably not inspire the same level of confidence that a domain like www.xyz.com would. Although e-commerce has been around awhile and most people are familiar with some aspect of it, a lot of people still don't trust the Internet. It's your job to prove that your small business deserves their trust and, once you have that, their money. Frankly, if you're not willing to pay 10 bucks a year to register an appropriate domain name, why would potential customers trust you to create valuable products or services? Your domain name is the first outward testament of your credibility.

Having an appropriate domain name can put you ahead of your competitors. Your domain name implies that you're also likely educated on emerging technologies. Using keywords in your domain name is a good idea, too. The search engines love that.

The right domain name is generally short and sweet. A descriptive and easy to remember name makes finding you easier for both customers and search engines. The easier you are to find, the more likely you are to attract business. Have you ever tried to find a business in a busy shopping district? Location, location, location.

Registering Your Domain

Check with Go Daddy, Register.com, or another web hosting company to see if your business name is available as a domain name. If so, buy it! Don't wait.

Register your domain name even if you aren't ready to use it yet. Treat it like gold. If you want to register your given name or a pseudonym and someone else owns it, you'll have to decide whether to call your business or just your domain by another name or go with a less popular suffix, such as .net or .biz. By the way, I would strongly suggest that you don't use hyphens and dots, especially if your name is owned by a competing business. It's too easy to err.

Protect Your Brand with Multiple Keyword-Rich Domains

Once you secure the right domain name—and do it as soon as possible—stay on top of renewal dates to keep it out of the hands of your competitors. Another great way to protect your brand is to secure more than one domain. It'll also increase your reach. Adopting a "keyword rich" domain strategy and looking for additional domains related to your business also helps. For example, if you are a baker and your delivery area covers a few different towns, you may want to purchase several domains, each incorporating the name of a different town: [name of town] bakery.com.

Domain names are investments. Considering that a domain is really an online storefront, it makes sense to invest in the best "location" you can afford. Domain values increase over time as domain authority grows. Domain authority is based on a few criteria.

The age of a domain lends to its legitimacy. An older domain is usually considered more trustworthy. Search engines will interpret your efforts to maintain your domain registration over a period of time as an indication that your business is not a shady operation. It's even better if you're the original owner and have maintained the registration for a website with traffic on that domain.

The size of your website gives your domain added authority too, because the number of pages on any domain expands that domain's ability to offer more useful content. Good content attracts natural links.

Search engines determine a domain's popularity by the number of back-links to sites with good domain authority. Because people link to sites that share similar content, back-links are a sign that the destination website is an authority in its area of expertise. Organic links generated through associations, social media, and so forth are the ones search engines take into account.

If your business is in a highly competitive industry, domain authority will be even more important. You may want to consider a premium domain name, with built-in authority. On the other hand, if your business is really micro-niched or has very little competition, you may not need to depend as much on domain authority and may do fine with a brand-new domain name.

Power Sites

One of the easiest and most effective ways for entrepreneurs to boost their Google ranking is through the use of .edu and .gov forums. These "power sites," if used correctly, can create a dramatic upward move in the rankings.

> ### POWER MOVE
> Boost your Google ranking with
> .edu and .gov forums.

For a traffic-generating, business building, outsourcing tip go to http://123Employee. com/outsourcesmart/interview/10, or scan this QR code and watch this video now.

QUALITY CONTROL
IN BAD TIMES

Some business managers are hesitant about using a virtual assistant because they don't know how they'll extricate themselves from the relationship if things go bad. But know this: you can protect yourself if a virtual assistant disappoints. In Chapter 4, we talked about setting up a VA contract. But there are other systems you can put in place to prevent human disaster and remove yourself from a soured business relationship.

HIRING MISTAKES

In your effort to begin outsourcing, you may be so overwhelmed and ready to delegate that you skip steps or gloss over important details during the hiring phase. It's a lot easier to do things right from the get-go than it is to go back and fix them later. Take your time.

She's Really Nice

One tempting mistake is to hire someone because you like him or her. Of course it's important to like your VA, but that isn't the reason you hire. Hire the most qualified person for the job, and build from there. Hiring someone for any other reason only sets you up for disappointment and sets up the employee to fail.

Dump and Run

This can happen to anyone. You're so anxious to get things off your plate, you just hand off a task without fully explaining it. You're busy, you don't have time. Then when the task is done wrong, you're upset. The person you've outsourced to might be skilled, but he won't have the chance to show you because he's not sure how to perform the task to your liking due to a lack of information.

Type A personalities are notorious for this unfair practice. They're stressed to the max to begin with, so when they get overwhelmed, they dump and run. Their providers are left in a quandary.

Expectations

Working with VAs can be such a great experience that you come to depend on them. One thing to keep top of mind when working with VAs: you're not the center of their universe. It's easy to forget they have other clients, unless, of course, you hire them full-time. Spontaneous tasks may be doable, but in some cases, they won't be. In order to be successful, VAs maintain a tight schedule with preestablished deadlines. Your VA might be in the middle of a project for another client when your "emergency" comes up, and she may not be able to drop everything and handle your crisis. Grant the same courtesy to other businesspeople as you would want them to grant you. Respect your VA's boundaries, and try not to get your feelings hurt if you can't get what you want exactly when you want it.

It's important to make sure expectations are understood by everyone on the project team. Be sure the people you delegate to understand what's expected, and that includes when the work is to be delivered. Such criteria should be set before the project begins, not halfway through.

Whether or not expectations are met, it's important to give feedback, especially as you and those you outsource to learn to work together. Just as more negative reviews are given for restaurant experiences than positive reviews, it's easy to fall into the trap of focusing on what's not working with your VA rather than what is. It's not always intentional. Positive experiences are oftentimes taken for granted, while feedback on shortcomings is handed out by the bucketful.

Avoid misunderstandings by making sure expectations are clear at the beginning of your relationship or at the onset of a project. When giving feedback, be sure to include what you liked along with details about things you'd like changed. This gives people a better understanding of what is expected so they can work toward doing things to your liking. As they learn to give you what you want the way you like it, it'll also save time on future projects.

Your Backup Plan

Even when expectations are clear, until you've outsourced a task or project, you won't know how a new person will work out. It's better to leave yourself an out. What's the worst that could happen? Plan ahead. The last thing you want to do is expect project completion on the same day the project is due to your client. You shouldn't even expect this from yourself. Life happens. Sometimes you just have to go with the flow.

When outsourcing a task, allow a cushion in case the work needs to be redone. You can decide whether to give the person you've outsourced to another chance or to look for someone else. Either way, build extra time into the schedule and refer to your backup plan. In some cases, that may be you.

Performance Reviews and Deadlines

Scheduling performance reviews and deadlines before the start of a project sets up the entire team for success. People perform better when they understand parameters, and as far as the deadline goes, it offers perspective. Even when directions are given and expectations made clear, people think differently, and it's good to know if you and the person(s) you outsource a project to are on the same page.

You may find the person you've outsourced a task to is moving in a slightly different direction than you'd planned. It's a good idea to check in during specific stages and request any necessary revisions as the project progresses. Projects can fail if there is a lack of communication between you and those you outsource to. You can avoid this in most cases by setting up checkpoints as you go along. Setting up these checkpoints before the project gets under way will allow both you and the person you outsource to peace of mind, knowing that resolution is possible during the process instead of upon completion. Revisions are much easier to make during the project, including revisions to completion dates and budgets.

In a worst case scenario, scheduled performance reviews will allow you to cancel a project if you feel that the service provider is not working out. Make sure you discuss this before you begin so there's no confusion.

Timelines

When you outsource a project, unless it's an ongoing service, most of the time you'll have a time frame and completion date in mind. Discuss this in advance with your VA in order to avoid mistakes and setbacks. Not only will a timeline be beneficial to you, but your service provider needs direction in setting aside the appropriate amount of time to complete the project. These details along with scheduled reviews should also be in writing.

Before you even decide to hire a VA, understand this: as you learn to work together, mistakes are going to be made, and disagreements may surface. Anticipate that these things will sometimes happen and you'll find it easier to deal with them as they come up. Expect perfection the first time, and you may be disappointed. Remain professional, and expect the same from your VA. Interview properly, test and focus on training, and you'll learn to love letting go.

For a traffic-generating, business building, outsourcing tip go to http://123Employee. com/outsourcesmart/interview/11, or scan this QR code and watch this video now.

QUALITY CONTROL IN GOOD TIMES

One of the biggest mistakes entrepreneurs make is ignoring their employees when things are going well. That's a recipe for things going bad. Behavioral psychology has shown that positive reinforcement encourages positive behavior. Have you ever noticed when someone compliments you on something you've done, or when they express gratitude, you want to do more for them? We're all motivated to excel when others take notice or show appreciation.

It works the same when you outsource to a VA. Service personnel have a built-in desire to please the people they serve. It takes a lot of energy to support others, and when you take notice, it refills their tanks. They naturally want to continue pleasing you. Take notice and acknowledge specific qualities whenever you can.

MANAGEMENT PRINCIPLES SPECIFIC TO VAs

You may be familiar with management principles in general, but you may not know those principles specific to working with outsourced virtual assistants. Because they aren't employees, they won't be motivated by the same things that motivate employees. They don't really work for you, so you can't "fire them." You can release them from service, but their livelihoods are not contingent upon your approval.

Managing one VA or a team can be easier without the complex dynamics associated with hired staff, but in some ways, it can be a little more challenging. Employees want to keep their jobs and are prepared to follow directions.

Whether you're working with employees or VAs, as a good manager, you've built rapport. You've made them feel as though the company's achievement is their achievement. Therefore, when the company succeeds, it's a reflection on the contributions they've made as part of the team.

Making Sure Your VA is Vested in Your Success

You're usually one of several clients your VAs are responsible to, unless they're working full-time for you. Building a relationship is an important element of forging a bond between you and your VAs, especially when they serve other clients. When your VAs feel bonded to you, they'll be vested in your success, and that investment will breed commitment. As team members, they'll want to please you and they'll also take pride in their work because they'll feel more connected to the project than someone just "doing a task" might be.

Acknowledge Your VA

When a task has been completed to your liking, be sure to hand out acknowledgment like candy on Halloween. Share feedback from clients with everyone involved. Everybody loves to hear positive feedback. In fact, studies show that acknowledgment has more value to people than monetary rewards. It sends a message that they're valuable. Even though we're *not* our actions, our self-worth is often connected to the value of what we produce. Acknowledgment makes people want to work harder the next time.

Try not to get so hung up on the expectation of success that you forget to acknowledge and reward a job well done. IBOs (independent business owners) with MLM (multi-level marketing) organizations work tirelessly for the opportunity to walk across the stage in front of their peers at company conventions. Those you outsource to will give you more if they know their efforts are appreciated.

You don't have to wait until a task is complete to reward those you outsource work to. If the project is a lengthy one with many stages of completion, encourage your team members with either verbal acknowledgment or small rewards. A thank-you card, a $5 Starbucks card, or a box of candy can be an inexpensive way to refill a tank that's close to empty. While you're at it, treat yourself.

Let's say you reach completion of a project and your team members exceed your expectations. A cash bonus—even a small one—will help sustain your relationship with members of your support team. And that, my friend, is the secret to successful delegation. You're on your way.

For a traffic-generating, business building, outsourcing tip go to http://123Employee. com/outsourcesmart/interview/12, or scan this QR code and watch this video now.

CONCLUSION

LIVING THE AMERICAN DREAM AS A SMART OUTSOURCER

With advancing technology and the dawning of the information age, new industries are emerging daily. Profitable niches are swollen with opportunity. If you're ready to launch your ideas, my hope in the time we've spent together, is that you're clear on the *why* of outsourcing smart. I've made it a point to adequately prepare you by filling in gaps in the *what to do* department and we're left with one more piece. *How* can you maintain a lifestyle of responsible affluence in an ever-shifting worldwide economy? As I've said, it's not only doable—it's easier than ever. There are a few points I'd like to emphasize before we part ways.

MANAGING TRAVEL EXPENSES

If you haven't guessed, this book is all about making money. But
affluence is no excuse for wastefulness. As you interface within
a global marketplace, domestic or international travel will be
likely. You should be managing and in many cases, writing off
your worldwide travel expenses. Here's another area you can
outsource as long as you're very clear and provide details.

Be sure to communicate the following to your VA:

Date and time. If you're a speaker or if you travel a lot, you
don't want to mistakenly double-book yourself. (This is also
important when you schedule appointments close to home.)
Make sure your travel arrangements between destinations
dovetail with the requirements. For instance, be sure you
don't book a red-eye out of Los Angeles if you need to be in
New York for a meeting at 9 a.m., unless of course you're
okay with going straight from the airport to the meeting
with little sleep and without a shower.

Budget. Let your VA know what your travel budget is before
arrangements are set in stone. Have a best case scenario and
a backup plan in case the ideal situation can't be met.

Airports. Do you like flying into Burbank, or would you
prefer LAX? You might even be okay with flying into
another city and renting a car if the price is right. Would
you rather have a window seat or an aisle seat? Back of the
plane or first class?

Accommodations. Which hotels do you prefer? Are there
any you absolutely won't stay at? What amenities would you
like? King or two queens? Do you have a specific site you
like to book on? Be sure the proximity of the hotel works
logistically with your meeting. It may not be worth the $20
you save if you have to contend with rush hour traffic.

The more information you provide, the better your VA can serve you and the less likely you are to be disappointed or, worse, to find yourself on a layover at a small airport drinking coffee from a vending machine.

Now, about that travel budget. Whatever you allocate, be sure it's within your resources and keep track of everything. You can manage your travel expenses the old-fashioned way by keeping a ledger, or, if you prefer, there are a bunch of web and phone apps designed to help you. Look for one that fits your personal needs. Some apps might be too complex, or they might be missing something that's essential.

You can always use an Excel spreadsheet to keep track of your travel expenses. Just log your account balances and spending. There are also templates on Google Docs for budget management. Your CPA might also suggest a viable alternative. If you have a preference for digital over analog, go in that direction, or vice versa. You've got to be comfortable with it to use it.

Tracking your spending is not only responsible behavior, it makes good business sense. You'll find out why at tax time. It'll also help you to stay organized if you spend your money in a variety of ways when you're on the road. If you always use your debit card, you can easily keep track. You know how much you have to begin with and how much you spend. But most of us also use cash and credit cards, sometimes more than one.

Balance your accounts! Knowing what you have to work with will help you avoid overdrafts and the fees that accompany them. One of my associates once received an overdraft penalty of $38 for a $1.95 cup of coffee. Ouch! Even if you can afford to lose the money, it's wasteful.

Keep accurate records in order to maximize write-offs. Unless you enjoy working with numbers, outsource the task to your bookkeeper. At the end of the year, he can e-mail a file to your CPA. You'll never have to touch it.

Write-offs

I love the sound of that word. With all the money that goes out the door to keep my business running, it feels really good to be able to write off some expenses. What this means is, in some cases you won't need to pay taxes on some of your money. You might be surprised by what you can deduct, depending on the business you're in. Any reasonable or necessary expenditure incurred to run and promote your business would be considered a possible write-off.

Anytime you travel for business, track your expenses. You can deduct travel expenses to trade shows, conferences, and seminars. Hotel costs can also be deducted. Meals can be a little tricky. Check with your CPA, but you should be able to write off lunches or dinners with business associates or clients.

How to Fly First Class at Business Class Prices

Book with a travel agent. They're allotted a certain number of upgrade vouchers. Also, you can request that the agent mark your reservation with OSI (other significant information). The record may indicate that you're a VIP, CEO, or other decision maker. If the agent thinks you could help him win your company's account, he might just give you an upgrade.

How to Access the Internet While Traveling

If you're "connected," you never have to leave your business. Of course, this is both good and bad. It's good if you enjoy your business, but constant connection can feel like a prison if you don't.

With domestic travel, in most cities you're usually assured an Internet connection in hotels and public places. But better safe than sorry: consider a wireless air card or hotspot just in case. They begin at about $50 a month, but they become priceless if you need to connect and there's no Wi-Fi.

Travel abroad also pretty much assures you a connection in most hotels, coffee shops, and even many bed and breakfast homes in most countries. There are also Internet cafes. You can't always count on uninterrupted Internet everywhere you go. Both Internet and electricity are sporadic in certain parts of the world, so be prepared—all the more reason to have a VA as backup.

Life-Enriching Charitable Causes

Enjoying your affluence doesn't always mean spending everything you earn. Living the American dream as a smart outsourcer means maintaining a lifestyle of responsible affluence as opposed to irresponsible indulgence. It's tempting for many who begin to reap the rewards of a successful business to increase their spending as their income goes up. Of course you deserve to have the things financial success offers, but do so responsibly. Continue to invest in growing your business, and remember to have a sound financial plan for the future.

One of the most satisfying things you can do is to give back to your community, your country, or your industry by participating in charitable causes. You'll soon find this practice to be both habit forming and life enriching.

Speaking of affluence, got another sheet of paper? At the top, write out your annual income. Place two zeros behind the current figure. You probably felt one of two things: exhilaration or fear, or maybe a combination of both. If you felt more fear, go ahead and take one of the zeros away. Feel more comfortable? That's okay. It's still 10 times what you're earning now. I'll bet you can handle that.

Since you're reading *Outsource Smart*, you're either curious or convinced that outsourcing can take your business to the next level, or you wouldn't be wasting your time. Either way, I guarantee by the time you get to the end of this book, you'll have new tools, new ideas, and a new attitude. That's what it takes to make changes.

Go ahead and look again at the number. If you took away a zero, decide if you want to add it back in. Either way, you're already ahead of the game. You've expanded your mind, and that's the first step toward your goal.

Quality of Life

The biggest advantage to outsourcing is improved quality of life. Otherwise, what's the point? The problem is many people go about it the wrong way. They set their sights on an outcome and give up before they give themselves a chance. A lot of times it has to do with worthiness. Do you believe you're worthy of wealth and success? I'm serious. Sit with the question awhile. The answer may surprise you.

Do you believe you deserve time to enjoy life, travel, buy the things you want, or whatever? If your head says yes but your heart says maybe not, count yourself among a great many people. You're not the only one. But that doesn't mean you need to stay there. You can decide right now that you want things to change. Choose differently and take the steps necessary to create a shift.

If you're working too hard, or if you'd like to influence your bottom line, outsourcing can help you meet your goals. The first thing to remember is you're not a victim. You have what it takes, and you won't have to risk everything to create the changes you want to see in your life. It's all about getting the information you need and applying it.

I wrote *Outsource Smart* for the person who's heard about outsourcing as well as the person who already sees the value in outsourcing and wants to know the best way to go about it. I've also included a section for those who want to begin outsourcing, and you can do both at the same time.

If you take one thing away from *Outsource Smart*, take this: life is not about sacrifice, everything you need is inside of you, and you're never too old to make changes.

Time and Money

It's tempting to define ourselves and others by what we do. She's a doctor. He's a teacher. Both are admirable professions and often on opposite ends of the pay scale. A worker in a manufacturing plant can make more than a teacher, and so can a gardener. Yet a teacher is usually held in higher esteem than either.

You're not what you do. And furthermore, what you do with your time isn't always in direct proportion with your income. If you're self-employed, how you spend your time and how you earn your money can be and often is totally unrelated. Just think of everything you do. Does a visit to the office supply store add to your account? Will you make more money today by posting on Facebook? Maybe indirectly, but if Facebook swallows you whole anytime you interact, you might want to consider its value.

Seriously, there are things you do every day that could be outsourced, freeing up time for you to do the things that directly impact your earning potential. The question is, if you knew what they were, would you do them? You might say yes, but are you sure you wouldn't let your fears or issues get in the way and prevent you from taking action?

The way to prevent this is to arm yourself with knowledge. It's easier to take action when you feel prepared. Life doesn't have to be hard.

Look at your projected annual income again. Is that what you want? That amount of cash (or more) written on your bank statement every month? I doubt it. I imagine you'd like to have the benefits that amount of money could buy, such as security, influence, and freedom. The money does you no good unless you can use it. Just ask someone who's waiting for a trust fund to mature. He may have a huge amount of money, but if he can't touch it, it does little good.

On the other hand, spending the best years of your life doing something you don't absolutely love, amassing resources you'll be able to tap into only when you're too old to enjoy them, makes no sense either. Wouldn't it be great to begin enjoying your life now, right where you are? A practical plan for outsourcing your business will not only help to increase your income, but also free you to spend your time doing things that bring you joy.

Money Is Not the Cure

There's no shame in wanting to make more money, and it's the key to unlocking many of your dreams. But it's not the solution to everything. If you're a miserable person being poor, being wealthy won't change that. If you're unmotivated or feel undeserving, the lack of money can be a scapegoat for not taking action in your life. Some people repel financial success subconsciously just to keep themselves down.

Guard your thoughts and watch your language. Avoid words like *someday*, *later*, and *in a while*—do *something* now. Regret is more painful than *redo*.

WHERE DOES MY BUSINESS END AND I BEGIN?

Self-employed people can all relate to having experienced varying degrees of confusion over the boundaries between their businesses and themselves. Are you confused too sometimes? Why? Have you forgotten you're the one drawing the line in the sand?

Don't be too hard on yourself. To some extent, we entrepreneurs all recognize the fuzzy borders that sometimes separate us from our businesses. People who work as employees usually don't have to deal with this, unless they're overachievers. They know that five o'clock is quittin' time, and they're watching the clock. For those who own their businesses, vigilance is the only defense.

Self-disciplined entrepreneurs have learned—sometimes the hard way—how to close the door on the home office at the end of a workday and leave their businesses behind until the next morning. Others are not even sure when their workday begins or ends, let alone how to let their businesses rest while they do *life*. People who work outside of the home have it a little easier, although boundaries between work and home can blur there too.

So what do we do about this, and why should we do it? Before you do anything, you have to want it. If you don't value your time, or if you'd rather do nothing else than work, go ahead and skip this section. You'll probably come back to it in a few years when you've finally had enough, but go ahead. But before you go, please read this next paragraph.

Even if we love what we do, it's important to take breaks from our businesses. Our emotional needs and responsibilities to our relationships are critical to living healthy, happy lives. Our bodies and minds require respite in order to recharge. Even a 15-minute break can help revitalize our resources. I know people who don't even take breaks or stop for lunch. That's a one-way ticket to burnout or illness. We're more productive when we walk away for a period and then step back into work. If you don't already do this, try it. You'll see the difference. Okay, now you can go if you still want to.

The most important reason to seek balance between our personal and business roles is quality of life. Is your family getting their fair share? If not, remember, you won't be able to go back and do it over again. Tomorrow you'll have to live with the choices you make today. Even if you decide someday to take things a little slower, you can't rewrite history.

When we feel good, we're happier. When we're happier, it's easier to think and be creative. Defining boundaries between work and pleasure allows us to express the fullness of life, and as we do, our products and services reach their full potential. No matter how you define it, that has but one outcome: success.

Outsourcing can help you, right here, right now. Delegate just one simple task and see how good it feels. It'll be a weight off your shoulders. Until you let go, you'll have no idea how heavy your load was. Straws do break camels' backs. Fifty-year-old people die from heart attacks, and even younger people suffer from exhaustion. Do you want to take that chance?

I'm going to believe that your answer is no. I'm going to have faith that if you cared enough about yourself to pick up *Outsource Smart*, there's a part of you that's ready to improve your life. Maybe you just want to check out outsourcing for the financial benefits. That's still okay, because I know once you begin living the laptop lifestyle, you won't ever go back.

What does quality of life mean to you? More time for your hobbies? Time with your family? You're going to have to be clear about what you want if you're going to work toward it. Quality of life is not a definition you can outsource. Its meaning is unique to you, and whatever it means is okay. Some people are so out of touch with the concept that they have no idea how to begin to characterize it for themselves. In case you find yourself there, here's a little exercise to help you define what quality of life might look like for you.

1. If you received a windfall and discovered you never had to work again, what would you do with your time? Would you travel, continue to work for pleasure, go back to college? Jot down some ideas and see what bubbles up.

2. What would an average *day in the life of you* look like? Where would you go? Who would you spend time with?

3. Remember your task list? Do the same thing—take a piece of paper and draw a line down the middle. At the top of the left side, write "Passageways," and on the right, "Roadblocks." In the left column, write the answers from the first two questions along with anything similar that

comes to mind. On the right, put anything you believe stands between you and the items on the left.

This exercise will provide a blueprint for picturing quality of life as it relates to your specific wants and needs. You'll probably continue to add to it as you begin to explore ideas. Imagination is a wonderful thing. Let yourself dream; pretend you can have whatever you want, and you'll inspire yourself to work toward it.

If the idea of greater freedom and joy appeals to you but you're not sure where to begin making changes, remind yourself that you only need to begin with the first step. Recognizing the "disconnect" will help you formulate the "reconnect." Choose. Life will take care of the rest.

Building Your Team

Stepping into a new reality can be scary, especially if you've recently started your business. You've already taken many risks and invested heavily in your success. Cash flow might be tight. The thought of spending money on outsourcing tasks when you could just "do them yourself" isn't the first thing on your mind.

Taking the outsourcing philosophy a step further and building a team might even be a bigger stretch. What you may not realize is that it's actually the one investment that will help sustain and manage your company's growth. Instead of seeing this as money going out, think of your team as an insurance policy for potential revenue. After you hire and train your team, you'll be able to make better choices with the time you've freed in your schedule. That's when the investment pays for itself—often many times over.

If you're going to maximize your success by outsourcing to a team, there are three basic support people you may want to begin with. Although there may occasionally be overlap, each one corresponds to specific tasks in a significant area of your business.

- **Administrative VA.** Responsible for all administrative tasks, billing, records, materials, e-mail management, etc.

- **Social media manager.** Social media updates, data collection, blog posting, list building, video, SEO, etc.

- **Customer service VA.** Database management, conflict resolution, relationship management, communications, etc.

If your administrative VA isn't good with numbers or doesn't know QuickBooks, I'd add a bookkeeper to the list. Your administrative VA can also serve as your social media manager if he is skilled in that area and has the time. These are all independent contractors who are usually dedicated to other businesses as well as yours.

There will also be providers you'll outsource to from time to time. These people will work directly with you or your VAs: web designers, computer techs, graphic artists, equipment repair people, or other professionals relating to your business.

As your business grows, your team may expand, depending on how much of your business you plan to outsource. Interestingly, even though each is an integral part of your business, team members may be on opposite ends of the world and may never interact, depending on their task assignments.

The next level of support, depending on your business, might find you adding these professionals to your outsourcing team:

- **Copywriter.** For newsletters, articles, web content, etc.

- **Marketing Strategist.** Advertising, social media marketing, press contacts, promotion, scheduling interviews, guest appearances, etc.

- **Sales Professional.** Product and service sales, fulfillment, phone support, telemarketing, appointment setting, etc.

Building a team you can trust will create a firm foundation for your business and provide you with the security you need to continue moving forward in your industry. Along with a business plan, integral to your success will be a solid interview process, appropriate training, and a system for retention so providers you enjoy working with are inspired to continue working with you.

Starting Your Own Service Business

Are you breaking your back building someone else's business? Have you been thinking about moving on and doing your own thing? Join the club! Over the last few years, many discontented employees are jumping ship to start their own businesses.

Whether they're taking advantage of new opportunities with Internet businesses, wetting their feet with direct sales, or dipping into sheer ingenuity and launching their ideas, people are seeing the advantages of working for themselves.

Some people feel they don't have a choice. Self-employment may be viewed as a survival strategy for some of the 8.2 percent of those who cannot find any other means of earning an income. For others, it may be seen as evidence of a desire to be one's own boss. How cool is that? Either way, opportunities are ripe for those willing to go after them.

Rising self-employment isn't restricted to the United States. In Great Britain, a recent news story at http://www.telegraph. co.uk reports that "resurgent self-employment soars to 75-year high." The latest business figures show a rise in self-employment not seen since the 1930s. Lots of people want to work for themselves. Though this may be the case, not everyone is ready to quit their jobs—financially, that is.

In your mind and heart, you may be ready to start a business. You may know exactly what you want to do. Your business plan may even show the likelihood of a profit in two or three years.

But you have bills that need paying today. So what do you do? Stay stuck? Sad to say, some people choose this route.

Outsourcing smart can help you create and run a business while you keep your day job. It's not unreasonable. If you're willing to put in a few extra hours a week working at your business, and willing to funnel some funds into an account that would support outsourcing a few projects, you might actually have that business up and running sooner than you think.

First, spend some time thinking about your current job. Do you really dislike it, or are you bored? Maybe you've outgrown it. If you really dislike what you do and don't think you'll get through another week without losing your mind, it might be better to think about doing something else. There's no point in spending eight or more hours a day doing something that makes you unhappy.

Maybe you really don't mind your job and would be willing to do it for a while longer. Think of a few strategies to survive. If you find your mind wandering often, ask your boss if you can have some more challenging tasks sent your way. This may be just what your company needs, and you don't know until you ask.

Let's talk about a few strategies to help you hang onto your job while you grow your business. Not all of these strategies will work for you. Every job has different options, and you are uniquely you. Try a few things, and don't worry about the strategies you don't feel comfortable with.

Ask for What You Want

Do you feel undercompensated for the work you do? It's hard to stay motivated when you feel as though you're working for less than you're worth. You've done everything you can to maximize the amount of money you make and—what's that? You haven't asked for a raise since you started with the company in 1492? What's stopping you from asking? If you're going to get what you deserve, you need to feel like you deserve it. Ask. You might be surprised. The worst that could happen is you find yourself right where you are.

If your boss said no to the raise, be sure to ask why. Would it make a difference if you were more credentialed? Ask if your company has a plan for training or continuing education. At the very least, you may come to enjoy your work more. Maybe that's what it takes to be considered for a promotion. Ask.

So many people are overlooked for promotions because their bosses have no idea they are interested. Make sure your immediate supervisor and her supervisor know you're interested in moving up the corporate ladder. It's okay to work a conventional job if that makes you happy; just make sure you know why you're there.

What motivates you to keep your job? A good salary? Benefits? Maybe the incentive to stay with it is the opportunity it will provide for you to invest in your business. A regular income will certainly make a difference as you outsource administrative tasks, follow-up phone calls, e-mailing, and social media updates while you're building your brand. Focus on the advantages it provides, and when the time is right, jump ship. If you've played the game strategically and used outsourcing to your advantage, there should be a little dinghy waiting to take you to your own vessel.

You're Ready to Outsource

I'm going to assume we already agree that any business can benefit from outsourcing certain tasks, okay? But how do you know when you've reached the point that outsourcing is critical to your success? There are a few indications that your business is not only ready to grow to the next level but also to reap advantages outsourcing provides. One of them is the fact that you're reading this book. On some level you feel ready. Nothing is a greater indicator than your intuition.

Outsourcing will allow you to work with a wider range of clients because you have a team working with you. If your company provides services, your team diversity will allow you to solicit and accept a wide variety of clients. If you create products, it may also allow you to accept more work. In seeking outsourcing professionals for your team, look for people with different qualifications and skill sets, which means you can even accept work you were initially avoiding because of your own limitations.

You won't be able to handle alone all the tasks associated with a growing business. Count on there being several areas in which you lack proficiency, not to mention the things that you just don't like doing. Outsourcing definitely helps you meet deadlines better than if you were doing everything yourself.

If you're thinking that it will cost you more money, in some cases, outsourcing is a means of reducing costs. If a particular service is expensive in your part of the world, you could work with a professional in another part of the world where that particular service is actually cheaper. It's not unusual for people in developed countries to outsource tasks and projects to developing countries, where the economic equation helps them manage tighter budgets.

Most importantly, when you work by yourself, making important decisions can be challenging. However, when you can consult with the intelligent professionals on your team, you'll find the process easier.

Barter Your Services

In case you hadn't noticed, bartering is making a comeback. Outsourcers and service providers are not only looking for ways to save money but also to advance their businesses through the old-fashioned art of trade. Assess your monthly expenses. If the economy has taken a big bite out of your resources, instead of cutting back, maybe you can find a way to exchange products and services with other businesspeople.

A VA can exchange administrative support for social media training. A writer can swap blog content for printing. If you're planning an event, you can offer exhibit space to the local newspaper in exchange for advertising. Your wallet doesn't need to dictate how you'll grow your business. If you're not sure you have the funds to begin outsourcing, think about what you do have. Would someone find value in it? If so, by all means, barter!

Bumps in the Road

Whenever you begin anything new, you're bound to hit bumps in the road. It's not a question of if, it's when. Starting a business is no exception. Preparation and innovation will help smooth your path as you progress, and one of the ways you can prepare is to put together a team of professionals in advance so when opportunities to grow your business come along, you'll have an established network of providers you trust to support you.

When you come across a stumbling block, step back and assess the situation. Remind yourself that things aren't always as they seem to be on the surface. By assessing what appears to be, you can determine your course of action. Could you outsource to a team member who would be able to handle the challenge? If you're prepared, you'll know exactly what to do and who to turn to for support.

Just Passing Go

I'm going to approach this section as if you're starting your business from the ground up. If you've already handled some of these details, skip over them and go to the next section.

The first thing you need when starting your outsourced business is a sound business plan. Think of it as a road map that'll help you arrange a series of actions coordinated with short- and long-term goals. Your business plan will allow you to look ahead, allocate resources, focus on your objectives, and prepare for problems and opportunities as your business grows. Something that always surprises me is the number of people who don't have a business plan. Don't be one of them.

One of the benefits of creating a business plan for your new business is its value as you're applying for business loans. But it's also vital for running your business, whether or not the business needs a loan or investors. You'll need a plan to optimize growth and development according to the priorities you set for your business. What this means is, not only will your plan serve as a road map, but it'll also act as a measuring stick to evaluate your progress.

We've now arrived at what might be your first opportunity to outsource a task. Your CPA or local Chamber of Commerce can refer a professional to help create your business plan, or you can look online. This can be expensive, so check out two or three resources before you decide who to work with. If you're going to tackle this on your own, there are easy-to-follow templates and software designed to help you create your business plan. Some are better than others, so look around.

After you know what you're doing, how to set it up, and what your end goals are, it's time to create your marketing plan. By the way, if you were thinking you didn't need a loan, you may reconsider when you get to this leg of the journey. Marketing can be costly. If budget is a consideration, your plan will probably lean more heavily on the Internet, social media, and other less expensive forms of marketing. Avoid making the same mistakes many inexperienced entrepreneurs make by neglecting to allocate a portion of your budget to marketing and promotion. The "If you build it, they will come" mentality has laid more than one potentially successful business to rest before their first year simply because they allocated no resources. If you build it, they *will* come—if you tell them who you are, where to find you, and how they'll benefit. Set yourself up for success by setting aside funds for marketing.

Choose a Business Name

What's in a name? A lot. Your name identifies your brand. Once you decide on your company name, you'll want to stick with it. Changing names isn't an option if you want to build on your branding and marketing efforts, especially with the Internet, as there are numerous web implications. Carefully consider what you'll call your business as it needs to work with your SEO.

Your name goes before you. First impressions are formed in seconds, and your name can either open gateways or close access to new clients. If your goal is impressing investors, you'll want to choose a name that will exude confidence and professionalism. Also, making your name web-friendly will impact your visibility.

When you're deciding on what you'll call your business, consider whether you want it to explain what you do. This can be like a one- or two-word commercial. Maybe you want a more abstract name that will draw attention. Will it be appropriate? What do you want your message to convey? Traditional values, contemporary creativity, or best price can all be reflected by your name.

A word about the global marketplace: make sure your name doesn't mean anything else in any other languages, because if you decide to do business globally, you may regret it. Then again, it may work for you depending on the service you want to outsource. Remember the Chevy Nova? It sold well in the United States, but fell flat on its face in Mexico. Why? Because in Spanish, *no va* means it doesn't go.

If you're a single-owner enterprise, you may want to use your name as your business name: Karen's Accounting Service, or

David Smith Enterprises. Keeping in mind that your name is your brand, you may name your business something you might want to change down the road. For instance, if you're a single woman and you marry, or a married woman who divorces, be sure you're comfortable keeping your business name even if yours changes.

Before you go out and buy stationery, buy the domain, if it's available. Register a DBA, and verify your right to use the name you've chosen. No trademark violations or copyright infringements are allowed. The last thing you need to do is find yourself in violation for using a trademarked name. Even if your birth name is Morgan Stanley or Jenny Craig, you may have to follow guidelines when naming your business.

Your Online Presence

Whether you decide to begin with a sales page, blog, or bona fide website, once you have your domain, you're ready. The easiest way to go (and a common alternative to a website) is a WordPress blog. It's simple, informational, and easy to maintain from the back end. You can get a free one at http://www.wordpress.com/, but I recommend you pay for a blog through http://www.word press.org/. You'll have control over your content. If wordpress .com should ever go away, your content would go with it. You can also design (or what's the magic word?) outsource your web design through WordPress. There are hundreds of templates to choose from at http://www.wix.com/, or you can have your site custom designed. What? Is html dead? No, it's still an option— more expensive, yet viable. WordPress is becoming more popular because it's user-friendly. Even Perez Hilton has a WordPress site.

Go Daddy, Bluehost, and Host Monster are all well-known web hosting companies. You'll pay somewhere between $5 and $10 a month.

As a service provider, you'll discover thousands of affiliate programs for products and services. If you are regarded as an expert in your industry, people will act on your referrals, and every month, you'll be paid a percentage of revenue generated. The number of hours you have in a given day is finite. When you're maxed, you're maxed. But affiliate programs allow you to continue to earn long after you pull down the shade and turn off the phone. You don't even need your own products. A middleman can earn a great profit.

When your website is ready to go live, if you haven't done so already, secure one or two e-mail addresses. Actually, you can use a different address for different aspects of your business. Depending on how organized you want to be, you can keep them all separate or funnel them into your main address.

Choose a Location

Where do you plan to work? Many service providers choose to work from home. Since you rarely meet with your clients in person, you may want to consider using the money you'd have spent on an office and invest it in your business instead. Even a cubicle in a shared office space runs at least a few hundred a month. That's your marketing budget! Make space at home if you can. If you need to meet with someone face to face, there's always Starbucks.

Other than the obvious (saving money, convenience, working in your pajamas), there are other benefits to working from home. Check with your CPA to see what tax credits and deductions are available. You can usually deduct a percentage of your rent and utilities.

If you've decided to work from home, make sure your work environment is conducive to *working*. Your clients will trust you to be efficient with the projects they outsource to you. Be sure to furnish your work space with essential equipment that works properly. Since you'll often be working with time-sensitive projects, be sure to have a backup plan in case your equipment fails or malfunctions, and limit opportunities for distraction. The better prepared you are to handle emergencies, the more success-ful you'll be and the more valuable to your clients.

Have a business phone or extra residential phone lines installed. A word to the wise: it's better not to use your home phone to accept incoming calls from clients. There are too many opportunities for mishaps and confusion, and if you have kids, well—I'll leave it at that.

Those who work from home will tell you one of the biggest challenges is not so much staying focused but closing down at the end of the business day. If you're going to avoid burnout, it's important for you to set boundaries with yourself and with your clients. Since you'll be working when you please—one of the rea-sons you work for yourself in the first place—be sure you set up breaks and schedule your work realistically. Clearly communi-cate your availability to your clients to avoid misunderstandings and faulty assumptions.

Licensing and Paperwork

Here's the not-so-fun part of starting your business. But I prom-ise, doing things correctly from the beginning will save you time and money later on. Even as a sole proprietor, you'll need to do some paperwork. Check to see what legal guidelines govern your industry. Are there any required business licenses or permits? Per-haps you can begin your relationship with outsourcing by del-egating to a qualified provider who will do the leg work for you.

Remember to research and file partnership or corporate papers if this is a joint venture. Reserve your corporate name if you will be incorporating, register or reserve a state or federal trademark, and register copyrights. Don't skip steps. It's easier to handle things at the onset than it will be to go back later and pick up what you missed.

While you're at it, check into business insurance. In some cases, errors and omissions insurance may also be a wise investment. It starts at around $23 a month, and you'll be working too hard in your business to allow a situation-gone-bad take it all away. Ask your homeowner's insurance provider if you can attach a rider to a homeowner's policy. While you're on the phone, ask about group health insurance options, another advantage to self-employment if you're married. It's worth looking into.

Almost There!

The paperwork's done. Your website's up and you have a phone. You're just a few steps away from being official. Go ahead and have business cards and stationery printed. Be sure to include your web address and e-mail address, along with your phone number. It's not a bad idea to include the link to your Facebook fan page, as long as you add fresh content and keep it current.

Time to open a bank account for your business. Before you ask: no, it's not okay to share your personal account with your business account. The IRS is becoming ever more critical, and red flags can send you reeling right into their radar. Which would you rather spend time on, developing a new product or service, or preparing for an audit? Although you can outsource certain tasks to your CPA, penalties for comingling funds, my friend, is something you'll have to keep for yourself.

Look for a business banker in your area, one that's convenient to your home, and open a checking account. Be sure to get overdraft protection. How embarrassing would it be to bounce a check to someone you do business with? If your credit is good, look into a line of credit so you always have funds available when you come across opportunities to expand your level of service. Pay it back as quickly as you can. The more you try to stay out of unnecessary debt, the better your chances of survival over the first few years in business.

Marketing Materials

If you plan to do street marketing or attend meetings and events to promote your services, consider whether you'll need brochures and other sales literature. If so, look for a quality printer. Here again, you may be able to barter services, so keep an open mind.

As a virtual service provider, most of your advertising will be done online, but you may still want to look into the cost of print ads or Yellow Pages advertising. The word on the street is that print media is on its way out. Maybe as an industry it is, but there are still specialty publications you might benefit from advertising in.

Church bulletins are a really inexpensive way to get the word out about your business. Although they're private and not where you might typically consider advertising, there are bound to be businesspeople in the congregation. Don't you think they'd be happy to do business with a company that supports their church bulletin?

A great way to get "free" advertising is to donate gift certificates as prizes for business functions and fundraisers. Offer one hour of complimentary service. There are a couple of advantages. First, it's good to support nonprofit organizations that provide value in your community. We shouldn't always be motivated only by "what's in it for me." However, these types of donations will also benefit your business.

Aside from receiving a tax deduction for giving a charitable donation, your business will be identified as a donor, and after you meet with the person who wins the gift certificate, he may sign on as a client. This is a great way to build your business. Even if the winner doesn't sign on with you, you'll be top of mind when someone asks for a referral for someone in your industry.

Build Your Database

If you attend trainings and continuing education seminars, which you should for several reasons, you'll hear this over and over: build your database. Your database is currency in today's marketplace. I already told you sales is a numbers game. Always was, always will be. When it comes to your database, the higher your numbers, the greater your potential to increase sales.

Your database is a list of names and contact information compiled as you interact with prospects online, at events, through networking, and via website traffic. Remember, these are people, not just bits of information. The better you service those in your database, the more likely they'll be to remain on your list, and the longer they're with you, the more opportunity you'll have to promote your services.

First, make sure you collect and store contact information in an organized manner. You may do this yourself or outsource to a VA. Even VAs have VAs. Use an Excel spreadsheet, and be sure to list only one piece of information in each cell.

For instance, each of the following elements goes in its own cell: first name, last name, business name, e-mail address, mailing address (which you might want to separate into city and state cells), website, and any other piece of information you'd like to track. It can be a big job if you haven't set up a database, but once you have a system, as long as you're disciplined, it's easy to maintain.

As a smart marketer, you'll use your database to communicate with your clientele and prospects. Send a newsletter out periodically, and include valuable information, news, and tips. The more value you provide, the less likely your followers are to unsubscribe. There are several programs you can use to interact with people on your database. If you're on a budget, Mail Chimp is free.

Outsourcing this task makes sense. It's busywork, and you're busy enough building your business. You can review your list anytime.

Ask and Connect

There's one more thing you can do to get the wheel rolling. You've heard it before, people are more likely to do business with people they know and like. Call everyone you know, and tell them you're in business. Ask if you can add them to your database. Ask them if there's anything you can do to help them. Ask for referrals. Ask for a testimonial. Just ask. Most people want to help others.

Connect with noncompetitors, and let them know about your new business. Ask how you can help them. Collaborate and joint venture. You might be a one-person show, but if you connect with other one-person shows to create a team, and each of you outsources to the other, you may all get a bigger slice of the pie!

Keep in mind, sales is a numbers game. The more people you know, the more times you reach out, the more people you let know about what you're doing, the more prosperous you'll be. Another thing to remember: you won't be able to go it alone. The greater your grasp of delegation and willingness to outsource to an overseas VA, the more smoothly your business will run. This is your business. Don't risk everything you've worked for.

Even with every detail in place, there'll be times you need to back up and move in another direction. Planning for these inevitable crossroads and being prepared to make different choices will keep your momentum at its peak.

The Crossroads

Your business, as an aspect of your life, will be a journey. Outsourcing, as an aspect of your business, can be seen the same way. As you learn to let go, you'll grow and evolve. You'll find yourself at many crossroads, times when decisions must be made, directions changed, or agreements altered. You'll be presented with choices along the way, and the impact of those choices will vary. You won't always have the answers, but your intuition will always be there to guide you.

Outsourcing isn't always just a means to an end. It can be exhilarating and enjoyable. I've said it many times in these pages: learning to delegate can be challenging at first, but the better you know yourself and what you're after, the more successful you'll be. As you come to trust your instincts and resist the temptation to repeat mistakes, you'll thrive, and your business will grow.

So when you come to a crossroads, think before you act, but don't think too long. Successful people make fast decisions. If they fall, they pick themselves up and begin again. You won't always make the right choices, but if you learn something and apply that learning, you've benefited.

Outsourcing will definitely change your life for the better even when some of your business relationships don't work out for whatever reason. Move on. Choose again. There will always be more positive experiences than not. Use them to remind yourself of the quality of life you enjoy by outsourcing smart.

A Work in Progress

If you're looking at business success as a destination, stop right here. It's a journey. Your business will morph and change many times as it grows, and the more up to speed you are with available options, the more advantages you'll have.

If we've met our goals, I've helped you see the value in outsourcing your business, and you have an idea of where to begin and the direction you'd like to move in. Not every suggestion in *Outsource Smart* will work for every business, just as having a butcher for an uncle means nothing if you're vegan. You may have been inspired to come up with new ideas that apply specifically to your business. That's great. The idea is to begin, wherever you find yourself on the path to success.

Apply your insights and review your answers to the exercises. Which of the Power Moves are you ready to begin implementing right now? The best way to create lasting change is to begin at the height of your inspiration and to move forward in absolute commitment to your goals. You may have never climbed a tree, but if a bear were chasing you, I'd bet you'd be able to scramble like a monkey!

Well, that bear is chasing you. Its name is Time, and it's running out. You'll never get back the hours, days, and years you've wasted on minutiae while micromanaging your business. Resist looking back at what you haven't done, and look straight ahead. Begin with the most doable elements of your outsourcing plan, and go forward from there. The more familiar you make yourself with the process of delegation; the more comfortable you'll be taking bigger steps toward more complex objectives.

There are hundreds of resources to support you as you begin to outsource smart. Working with overseas VAs will help you step into this world quickly and affordably. Use what you've learned from this book to guide you in seeking the right professionals, and build from there.

No matter how involved you become with outsourcing, always remember this: you, as a human being, have been gifted with reason and an inner knowing that acts as a barometer in all the actions you will ever take. You have what it takes inside of you to move yourself to the next level. The knowledge you seek will enhance what's already there. Merge this with a capable, well-trained support team, and you've got the world in your hands.

For a traffic-generating, business building, outsourcing tip go to http://123Employee. com/outsourcesmart/interview/13, or scan this QR code and watch this video now.

INDEX

PROPERTY OF
SENECA COLLEGE
LIBRARIES
NEWNHAM CAMPUS